BUSINESS, POLLUTION AND REGULATION

CONTENTS

FOREWORD

It must seem to many people that almost everything that can be said about 'the environment', from rain forests to waste, has been said: and so stridently that we would believe our very selves to be redundant in the face of nature. Neither proposition is true. Though much has been said, we actually know very little, in particular about the critical issues of the environment, which are climate change, changes in biological diversity and the impact of human activities on the functioning and inter-relationship of ecological systems.

The environment is an aggregation and synthesis of so many components, not least of which is human population, that the understanding of ecosystems or species function does not reside in any particular discipline; ascribing cause to effect is inspired frequently by idealism supported only by contradictory or inconclusive science and unmoderated by reality.

True science proceeds from intelligent observation, leading to hypothesis, data gathering, interpretation and validation (repeatable experiments). First order research is essential for assessing the validity of propositions that affect policy and law-making and having a bearing upon our global living quarters.

There is at least one proposition that is self-evident: we must value nature and respect her bounty. There is nothing valueless in nature and neither is it given to us to distinguish unequivocally between absolute and relative values. Thus, we witness daily the transformation of one ecosystem to favour another, less pristine, to serve either the basic needs of expanding human populations or the predations of industry.

To some, human welfare is the correct sacrifice to nature. A little more realistic and constructive observation reveals that nature has endowed men and women with the facility both to exploit and to sustain: and the better reconciliation of these actions must be the common quest of science and public policy.

The ethos of this work, about managing pollution, is that better science will ameliorate the demands for a pollution-free biosphere, that a higher degree of tolerance will be discovered for many substances than current strictures permit; obversely, society will tolerate less and less levels of ill-health and environmental degradation from poisoned land, air and water than presently allowed or condoned.

'Pollution' begs several questions. Not least is whether global warming, as predicted, can be arrested or modified by reducing emissions of greenhouse gases. Another question, from a local perspective, is 'How clean is clean?', taking into account the characteristics of a particular industry, its siting, its impact or value to local and neighbouring communities, the nature of substances discharged into which media and the rate of dispersion and eventual residence. As to definition, pollution has a canvas larger than effluents and emissions from industrial processes: pollution is the introduction of any substance or activity that depauperates human health and the functioning of an ecosystem. From measuring and monitoring the impact of industrial emissions on air, land and water, we can observe the industrial, agricultural and social dimensions of climate and biological change and their implications for human health.

Speaking as a botanist, it pleases me that routine control of effluents and emissions is of the very essence of the UK biodiversity action plan (following the UNCED Biodiversity Convention, 1992) aimed at the protection of some 1,250 species of plants, birds, mammals, insects and amphibia presently at risk in the United Kingdom. That most of these species are known only to naturalists and the scientific community is a situation that is rapidly being altered by the huge amount of resources targeted at schools and places of higher education in strategies to ensure that environmental awareness and expertise permeate politics and the economy long into the future.

This book is about pollution but it is not the authors' intention to do other than explore grounds for responsible pragmatism in environmental management, map out the likely direction of pollution prevention and eschew dogma.

Although many of the ideas expounded in this book are directed at corporate women and men (usually the so-called SMEs, or small to medium-size enterprises that have yet no formal environmental philosophy) its aim also is to spur on the efforts already being made by companies formally and practicably committed to improving their environmental performance. But it is SMEs that in aggregate contribute most to the sum of pollutants. I believe that by thinking and acting locally on environmental impact the global issues will take care of themselves.

Professor David Bellamy

ABOUT THE AUTHORS

Struan Simpson's interest in the environment comes from a background in public health. He advises on the international regulation of safety and the environment and has wider interests in Third World development. In the 1960s and 1970s Struan spent several years in West Africa organising family planning programmes for the Ford Foundation and was awarded a Fellowship to the University of California at Berkeley in recognition of his work on infant feeding in Nigeria. Until recently, when he began to take a close interest in ecology, Struan worked as an independent consultant to the offshore oil industry, contributing to the development of an international basis for comparing accident data and representing the industry at the International Maritime Organization.

Struan lives with his wife Jean and two children in London.

Jacqueline Carless is an independent consultant specialising in environmental management. Her interest in environmental matters began in her native Canada where she worked on waste management issues. Since her migration to Britain, she has worked with many organisations ranging from university departments to blue chip companies. In addition to this book, Jacqueline's recent and current work includes the development of environmental procurement specifications and corporate environmental reports, writing and editing a company environmental newsletter and assessing the environmental merits of products ranging from soaps to nappies.

Jacqueline lives in Brighton with her husband Ben and two sons.

ACKNOWLEDGEMENTS

The authors would like to acknowledge Jess Holroyd for permission to publish Figures 3.1 and 3.2, Technical Communications Ltd for permission to publish Figure 4.2.

They also thank Evette Carless for her assistance with database design.

LIST OF TABLES

LIST OF FIGURES

1. BUSINESS AND THE ENVIRONMENT

Europe's two-hundred year industrial legacy is a generally improved standard of living, universal access to goods and services, cheap energy and an ageing population. Economic growth among 355 million Europeans living in the West and a further 425 million living in Eastern Europe and the former Soviet Union, notwithstanding peaks and troughs, is predicted to continue at around 2–2.5% annually, if any faith is to be put in economists and politicians.

Step-by-step we are beginning to acknowledge the finite nature of natural resources and to recognise the need for technical and managerial skills that reconcile the demands of people as consumers to the demands of nature as provider, to improve the quality of life of our own generation in ways that can be sustained.

Taking a historic perspective on pollution and public health, a three day London 'smog' (a frequent winter post-war phenomenon, comprising smoke from coal fires, sulphur dioxide and fog) in 1952, caused the deaths of around 4,000 people and led to a ban on burning coal in open hearths and the introduction of controls on industrial emissions.

Extreme events and high mortality (Flixborough, Piper Alpha and the Kings Cross disaster) and the metamorphosis of a robust Health and Safety Executive (HSE) has put health and safety firmly on the industrial balance sheet, into business culture and public consciousness. The environment is not yet as firmly entrenched in business, politics or public opinion, except among the larger companies (with high consumer profiles and competitive axes to grind) and also among environmental professionals and 'green' activists.

The setting up of the new Environment Agency in England and Wales (EA) and the Scottish Environment Protection Agency (SEPA) may well have brought pollution prevention and control into managerial focus. More recently, there has been a swell to account for the negative effects of the energy cycle on health, safety and the environment. Neither public nor private balance sheets yet account for the external and consequential costs of lost time resulting from mortality and morbidity arising from pollution. Nor has any value been ascribed to life-sustaining natural assets (habitats and species). Costs to industry are not the penalties imposed by the courts but those associated with capital and revenue expenditures to meet the requirements of the Water Acts and Integrated Pollution Control (IPC), obtaining planning consents, the siting of industry and making provision for contingency liabilities.

Among the constraints to optimal environmental performance is the energy market: control of 'greenhouse gases' is dependent on the energy market, on the oil price relative to gas, coal and nuclear power. While we can trim fat in the West, most of the rest of the world's population aspire at least to modest affluence as their economies come on stream. But even in our own day-to-day pollution management, many companies regard prevention as a damage limitation exercise where compliance is the extent of environmental commitment.

Others reach beyond compliance into voluntary standards for energy consumption, waste recycling, emissions to air, water and land, and by adopting environmental management systems (for example, British Standard 7750 and the Environmental Management and Audit Scheme (EMAS)), even in the absence of sector specific codes of practice. Routine management, measurement and monitoring are perceived as being expensive and time consuming. But cost effectiveness can be managed as a function of site location, the nature of the local ecosystem, rate and fate of pollutant dispersion and the viability of the enterprise in relation to penalties and remediation.

While larger companies can internalise the costs of pollution prevention and control by increasing the prices of goods and services, smaller enterprises may decide that the risks of being prosecuted are worth taking. It is often the smaller companies which lack the wherewithal or technical skills required for self regulation and who fall outside of Integrated Pollution Control (IPC).

For example, the printing industry, composed mainly of small businesses employing less than 10 people, outside the remit of IPC and believing themselves immune from European law, still tend to follow traditional methods of effluent treatment and disposal, i.e., discharging silver and other effluents to the public drains. This happens in the majority of cases despite the liability of companies and company directors to fines of up to £20,000 per offence in the magistrates' courts or unlimited fines and imprisonment in the Crown Courts.

Major companies in the oil, metal and chemical sectors, classified as 'dirty', have made considerable progress in cleaning-up, as a consequence of legislation and stakeholder (shareholders, employees, customers, suppliers) demands for:

- Risk and liability aversion

- Anticipating regulatory changes

- Socially aware 'corporate citizenship'

The state of being 'green' thus extends beyond the simple control of effluents and emissions to a broader sense of social responsibility. 'Greenness' needs to become part of the corporate culture, akin to health and safety, and adding a new dimension to the law of the business jungle.

Even so, in 1995, after hundreds of prosecutions under the Water Acts and 'ratcheting-up' standards under the 1990 Environmental Protection Act by Her Majesty's Inspectorate of Pollution (HMIP) and local authorities, the main obstacle to compliance has been corporate reluctance to make the necessary and expensive structural adjustments to meet 'green' criteria.

Adjustments are being made nevertheless, to scales that accord to company size. Large 'dirty' companies within IPC and those with direct consumer contact recruit environment specialists or retain consultants. Small to medium-size enterprises (SMEs) do not have the resources of their big sisters and must rely upon consultants and trade and professional associations. In the medium to long term, pollution prevention will prove not only to be legally prudent but will help SMEs retain their independence.

SMEs, outside the rigours of IPC, but subject nevertheless to regulation by local authorities, appear reluctant to acknowledge the aggregate impact of their relatively small discharges on general water quality. Taken collectively, the volumes of oily wastes, sludge and heavy metals from SMEs is greater than from the traditionally large dirty industries that come under the scrutiny of the Environment Agency (EA) and green activists.

Implementation of IPC by local authorities will broaden the application of PPP (the Polluter Pays Principle). SME survival will depend upon avoiding potentially debilitating penalties by the timely adoption of abatement technology and process adjustments. Other strategies, devised as national policy and imposed by the local authorities might include payments other than fines, as 'permits to pollute' or new systems of corporate taxation.

Tradeable pollution permits for companies discharging effluents into specific rivers or river stretches were widely discussed in late 1995, and are similar to permits for sulphur emissions from power stations (see the discussion on the proposed Carbon Tax in the Energy and transport section of Chapter 2).

In a permit scheme, the pollution regulator lays down limits for emissions or discharges and issues the permits to each company. A company discharging less than the permitted level may then sell the excess to a company that needs this extra capacity. Companies may need extra capacity permanently, because of expansion, or temporarily, due to difficulties reducing emissions to the permitted levels.

Health, safety and the environment

Health, safety and the environment are closely linked. Many substances that threaten employee health also damage the environment. There are some exceptions: for example, carbon dioxide, a by-product of fossil fuel combustion and the principal 'greenhouse' gas. Excessive carbon flux, while affecting climate in ways yet to be clarified, does not present a direct health hazard except in extreme cases.

Health and safety is now well established in the structure of business; 'the environment' is more often than not an add-on to the job specification of the health and safety manager. As the intrinsic nature of health and safety to business was emerging in the 1970s and 1980s, companies often argued that they could not afford the burden of extra and 'unnecessary' regulation and that they could adequately protect their employees without them. The speciousness of these arguments became manifest as accident, industrial morbidity and fatality rates persisted.

Insistence on regulation and inspection, particularly of the highly resistant offshore oil industry, *inter alia*, have brought about reductions in injuries and fatalities, both from improved management and the introduction of less labour intensive technology. Health and safety have now become firmly entrenched in the industrial culture of the traditionally high accident prone construction and mining sectors. Similar persistence by the pollution inspectorates, public pressure, high costs of litigation, compensation and insurance and risk averse lending policies should also ensure that the environment, too, becomes an established business ethic.

Industrial health and safety gained from regulation, inspection, the abolition of personal 'safe harbour' and the growing threat of litigation, but little public interest. The environment to a greater degree has caught the public imagination.

In England and Wales, the Department of the Environment (DoE) prefers that companies operate beyond the minimum legal requirements, thus avoiding the necessity of costly litigation and inspection: in other words, de-regulation.

In late 1993, DoE 'invited' the packaging industry to address itself to an objective of recovering 50-75% of packaging wastes by the year 2000, without legislation, submitting its proposals to the Department by 1995. Spurred by such a challenge, the industry in coalition produced a plan which was accepted by the Environment Secretary in October 1994.

Similarly, European Union legislation of health, safety and the environment, acknowledges costs, aims at harmonisation of actions among member states, the 'level playing field' and seeks national self-regulation beyond simple compliance. Voluntary measures, such as the Eco-Management and Audit Scheme (EMAS – see also BS7750), encourages industry to manage uniformly, monitor and control environmental impact in appropriate ways outside the scope of legislation.

Insurance and environmental risk

A number of the larger European insurance companies led by a United Nations Environment Programme (UNEP) steering committee, are seeking to establish environmental performance criteria as a basis for calculating insurance premiums. The initiative is being led by Uni Storbrand, a Norwegian insurer and involves General Accident in the UK, Gerling of Germany and Swiss Re. They also plan to recruit other insurers who share their concerns about increased risks associated with climate change, groundwater contamination, acid rain and oil spills.

Sustainable development

Sustainable development is achieved when the needs of human populations are provided for within the constraints of finite natural resources and taking account of the future.

The United Nations Commission on Environment and Development (UNCED) defines sustainable development as development that 'meets the needs of the present without compromising the ability of future generations to meet their own needs'.

A sustainable society is one which manages its resource base in much the same way as stable, subsistence farming traditionally would be conducted. It observes change, adopts appropriate technology (albeit low-intermediate) and techniques that make provision for successive seasons.

Sustainability is defined in principles promulgated by the World Conservation Union (IUCN), the United Nations Environment Programme (UNEP) and the World Wide Fund For Nature (WWF). See Appendix I for their nine principles of sustainable development.

Limits to sustainable economic growth

Limits to growth need to be considered in the relationship between politics and economics and the population-resources-environment crisis: a debate which had its first airing at least twenty-five years ago when the main elements of the present crisis were anticipated at the first global environmental conference in Stockholm (1972).

The possibilities for economic growth in a finite world, the quality of growth in an expanding market (i.e., the EU internal market) against widespread disparities in income were reiterated in the declarations of the Treaty of Rome. It was clear then as now that reconciliation between economic growth, environmental quality and quality of life will remain elusive and an illusion until this disparity between Organization for Economic Cooperation and Development (OECD) countries and the rest of the world is headed towards a solution.

Meanwhile, economic growth in Europe continues to be of an unreconstructed kind having adverse environmental impact. Road freight, car ownership and tourism increase; commercial and domestic building expand; increased economic activity and consumption lead to more roads, land-use pressure, air pollution, resource depletion and waste.

Paradoxically, growth-led economic stability in Europe and OECD is a pre-condition of world-wide sustainable growth, to competitiveness and improved living standards among the countries in economic and political transition, in Africa, Asia, Latin America and the republics of the former Soviet Union (FSU).

NGOs in the system

It is the official policy of developed and developing countries to encourage and support non-governmental agencies (NGOs) in the non-profit sector, to represent community and special interest groups (for example, Friends of the Earth (FoE) and Greenpeace among environmental activists groups; Royal Society for the Protection of Birds (RSPB) among wildlife and naturalists' trusts), in the policy-making process, on occasion funding them to undertake tasks which they themselves have identified and to conduct programmes of public education. Funding rarely extends to the provision of 'core' support, since in the true British democratic parsimony, the public is also expected to make the greater contribution. Industry too sustains NGOs to quite a large extent, in its funding of surveys, conservation and community initiatives.

In 1995 Friends of the Earth (FoE), RSPB and WWF introduced a 'green gauge' index to measure river pollution, rural land loss and biodiversity, which is proposed for presentation as an annual survey of key environmental indicators. A fair proportion of FoE's (and Greenpeace's) work is to present alternatives to the official version of improvement and progress in the environment. Thus, controversial science is put to the task of confrontation. Recently, Shell's plans to dispose of the concrete Brent Spar oil storage platform into the ocean stimulated another conflict – that between 'science' and public sentiment. In this case, public sentiment was misled by sloppy science. Shell's climb-down and subsequent vindication of its original position illustrated this.

Environmental NGOs can be classified as independent (membership subscriptions and fund raising) critics of government and industry (Greenpeace and FoE); those that rely on government and industry project funding (WWF); independent (membership subscriptions) advocacy organisations such as RSPB; unaffiliated independent project groups (Living Earth); and special interest bodies such as Business in the Environment and the Conservation Foundation.

Further reading

Elkington, J., P. Knight and J. Hailes *Green Business Guide: How to Take Up – And Profit From – The Environmental Challenge,* Victor Gollancz Ltd, 14 Henrietta Street, London, 1992

Environment business magazine, Information for Industry, London, 1994 –

Flood, M. *Business and the Environment,* 21 Church Lane, Loughton, Milton Keynes MK5 8AS: Powerful Information, 1995

Gilbert, M.J. *Achieving Environmental Management Standards: A Step-By-Step Guide to Meeting BS7750,* Pitman Publishing, 128 Long Acre, London WC2E 9AN, 1993

Hawken, P. *The Ecology of Commerce: How Business Can Save the Planet,* Weidenfeld and Nicholson, The Orion Publishing Group, Orion House, 5 Upper St Martin's Lane, London WC2H 9EA, 1993

Hillary, R. *The eco-management and audit scheme a practical guide,* Business and the Environment Practitioner Series, 100 High Street, Letchworth, Herts: Technical Communications (Publishing) Ltd., 1993

Rogers, M.D. (Ed.) *Business and the Environment,* Macmillan Publishers, 1995

Shrivastava, P. *Greening Business: Profiting the Corporation and the Environment,* Thomson Executive Press, Cincinnati, Ohio, 1996

United Nations Environment Programme (UNEP) *Company Environmental Reporting: A Measure of the Progress of Business & Industry Towards Sustainable Development,* UNEP Industry and Environment Programme Activity Centre, Paris, 1994

Welford, R. *Earthscan Reader in Business and the Environment,* Earthscan Publications, 1996

2 ENVIRONMENTAL ISSUES

A scientific consensus has set out those environmental issues that are pressing in the global, regional or local context, even though cause and effect are still uncertain in many important areas such as carbon flux and climate, the capacity of the environment to degrade pollutants, chemical effects on the human organism, the identification and role of key species in maintaining biological diversity, and so forth. Less consensus attaches to nuclear power on account of the difficulties in reconciling scientific, political and community perceptions of acceptable risk.

The purpose of this chapter is to provide an overview of the relationship between these issues, legislation and corporate responsibility, in the UK and in Europe.

The following subjects are covered in this chapter:

- Air, land and water

- Chemical spills and industrial accidents

- Conservation and biodiversity

- Energy and transport

- The marine environment (coastal pollution; the North Sea)

- Noise

- Nuclear energy

- Wastes

Air quality

Urban air quality and public health in the UK's industrial cities improved dramatically following the Clean Air Acts (1956 and 1968) with the consequent restrictions on domestic and industrial coal burning leading to reduced levels of smoke and atmospheric sulphur dioxide.

Poor urban air quality today is now associated with an increase in sulphur, nitrogen and carbon oxides, lead, benzene and particulate levels from vehicle exhausts.

The air pollution dilemma is further complicated by the fact that upon emission, certain chemical reactions can occur causing the formation of secondary pollutants. The primary pollutants include sulphur dioxide and carbon monoxide – these are directly emitted by industry and from car engines. However, it takes a series of rather complex reactions, involving several other pollutants and the presence of sunshine, to form ozone which at ground level is a serious human health problem. This makes control strategies for ozone and other secondary pollutants difficult.

Air pollution creates dirt, grime and urban soiling. Diesel engined vehicles have replaced coal as the main source of smoke and particulates in cities, blackening structures, permeating buildings with dust and contaminating soil and water.

The main pollutants affecting air quality and health are:

- carbon monoxide

- metals

- nitrogen compounds

- organic compounds

- oxidants

- particulate matter

- sulphur compounds

Tables 2.1 and 2.2 illustrate sources and impacts and identify air quality issues of global and national importance.

Fleet management is a positive option for energy saving but the arguments surrounding leaded vs. unleaded petrol and diesel fuel vs. petrol only add to the dilemma of companies wishing to select clean air options. Some practical measures to reduce the impact of motoring on the environment is journey management and ensuring that vehicles are well maintained.

Recently (early 1995), the UK Department of Transport introduced roadside checks of vehicles suspected of exceeding legal limits for carbon monoxide, volatile organic compounds (VOCs) and particulates and have introduced tougher MoT test standards from September 1995. Penalties include fines of up to £2,500 and the prospect of an immediate ban.

Further reading

Bertorelli, V. *Air Quality A to Z: A Directory of Air Quality Data for the United Kingdom in the 1990s*, Department of the Environment, PO. Box 135, Bradford, West Yorkshire BD9 4HU, 1995

QUARG *First Report of the Quality of Urban Air Review Group*, Quality of Urban Air Review Group, Department of the Environment, PO. Box 135, Bradford, West Yorkshire BD9 4HU, 1993

Zanetta, A. *Air Quality Indicators for Environmental Impact Assessment*, Commission of the European Communities Institute for Systems Engineering and Informatics, European Commission, 1994

Table 2.1 Global and regional air quality issues, their sources and environmental impacts

Issue	Main pollutants	Sources of pollutants	Description of issues and environmental impacts
Global warming or the greenhouse effect	Carbon dioxide (CO_2), carbon monoxide (CO), sulphur dioxide (SO_2), nitrogen oxides (NO_x), hydrocarbons, particulates, polycyclic hydrocarbons and fly ash. Chloroflurocarbons (CFCs), Methane (CH_4)	Fossil fuel burning, transport, burning trees and crops. Used mainly as a refrigerant. Biological breakdown.	Carbon dioxide is the most important "greenhouse gas". The greenhouse effect or global warming describes a theory that the accumulation of CO_2 in the atmosphere may lead to warmer temperatures all over the earth. It is expected that due to global warming the climate may become more extreme, agriculture is likely to be affected (with many areas that are currently arable becoming too hot and humid and currently non-arable land becoming economically productive) and sea-levels may rise causing flooding in many parts of the world, including in the Netherlands and Bangladesh.
Stratospheric ozone depletion	CFCs, 1,1,1-trichloroethane, Halon Methyl chloroform Carbon tetrachloride	Used mainly as a refrigerant. A solvent. A fire extinguishant. A solvent and cleaning agent. Used to make CFCs, also a solvent (but not in UK).	Ozone at ground level is a pollutant; in the stratosphere, ozone shields the earth from ultra-violet (UV) radiation from the sun. Strong UV radiation can damage cell structures and exposure is expected to cause an increase in the incidence of skin cancer and cataracts in both humans and animals.
Acid rain	Sulphur dioxide (SO_2) Nitrogen oxides (NO_x)	Sulphur oxides released from fossil fuel burning become oxidised in air after their release. As above, plus transport.	The gases released from power stations and industry containing SO_2 and NO_x combine with water vapour and fall with the rain as dilute acids. Dry deposition (as dust particles) also occurs. The gases travel great distances before they are deposited, thus, Britain produces much of the pollutants responsible for the acid rain damage in Scandinavia. Acid rain causes the death of trees, the poisoning of lakes and the corrosion of buildings.

Adapted from: Yearley, S. *The Green Case: A Sociology of Environmental Issues, Arguments and Politics*. Harper Collins Academic, 77-85 Fulham Palace Road, Hammersmith, London W6 8JB, pp. 11-46 and Jones, G., Robertson, A., Forbes, J., and Hollier, G. *Collins Dictionary of Environmental Science*. William Collins Sons & Co. Ltd., 8 Grafton Street, London W1X 3LA, pp. 3-4, 203-204, 318.

Table 2.2 A description of the most important pollutants affecting air quality in the UK

Pollutants	Sources (in order of decreasing importance)	Trends	Environmental and human health impacts
Nitrogen oxides (NO_x)	Road transport, power stations, industry, heating and incineration.	Increasing due to increasing road transport.	Damages plants and irritates the human respiratory tract. Also important for the formation of photochemical smog and acid rain.
Sulphur oxides (SO_x)	Power stations, industry, domestic heating, other heating and vehicle emissions.	Decreasing due to improved pollution control.	Contributes to acid rain, damages plants and the human respiratory tract.
Carbon monoxide (CO)	Road transport (85%), domestic heating, power stations and industry.	Increasing due to increased road transport.	Reduces oxygen-carrying capacity of blood, can be especially important in areas with heavy traffic.
Particulates	Main source used to be coal burning, now is diesel-engined vehicles.	Increasing due to increased number of diesel-engined vehicles on the roads.	Combined with SO_2 to produce London's smogs, leading to the deaths of 4000 over a 4 day period in December, 1952. Act as a carrier taking toxins deep into respiratory tract. Reduce visibility.
Volatile organic compounds	Road transport, power generation and industry.	Increasing with road transport.	Important for local air quality and in the formation of photochemical smogs.
Metals (arsenic, cadmium, chromium, copper, lead, mercury, nickel and zinc)	Power generation, industry, road transport and incineration.	Stable.	Levels highest in urban areas, especially those with heavy traffic.
Ozone (O_3)	A secondary pollutant formed by a complex series of reactions involving hydrocarbons, nitrogen oxides and sunlight. The precursor chemicals are emitted in vehicle exhausts but ozone tends to be swept downwind from city centres resulting in elevated ozone concentrations in suburban and rural areas.	Increasing in urban areas due to the use of catalytic converters (prevent the emission of nitric oxide which destroys ozone).	Damages crop plants and harms the human respiratory tract.
Toxic organic micropollutants (TOMPS)	Mostly transport-related. Also industry, incineration.	Increasing due to increased vehicular transport.	Many have serious health implications, including PCBs (reproductive failure in birds, suspected to cause sperm count reduction in humans) and dioxins (linked to birth defects and a suspected carcinogen).

Adapted from: Harrison, R.M. *Pollution: Causes, Effects and Control*, Royal Society of Chemistry, Thomas Graham House, Cambridge CB4 4WF, 1992, pp.127–156 and QUARG, *Urban Air Quality in the United Kingdom*, First Report of the Quality of Urban Air Review Group (QUARG), Air Quality Division, Department of the Environment, Romney House, 48 Marsham Street, London SW1P 3PY, 1993, pp. 3–27.

Contaminated land

Contaminated land has the potential of causing harm to human health, other living creatures or of polluting water. It is mostly associated with decommissioned refineries, coal mines, petrol stations, chemical processing sites and abandoned waste tips, *inter alia*. The latter have produced some notorious cases of poisoning and other hazards from the emission of noxious, toxic and/or explosive gases.

Table 2.3 Industries and processes associated with land contamination

Mining and extractive industries
Iron and steel works
Metal treatment and finishing
Chemical and pharmaceutical industries
Oil refining and storage
Timber treatment
Railway land, especially large sidings and depots
Scrap yards and fragmentation plants
Paint and dyestuff industries
Sewage works and farms
Application of sewage sludge to agricultural land
Fly-tipping, cable-burning and bonfires
Waste disposal (hazardous and non hazardous industrial and household wastes)
Dockyards and filled dock basins
Electrical goods manufacturing, e.g., use of solvents and metals
Deposition of air pollutants, e.g., vehicle emissions

The Department of the Environment (DoE) at present estimates that the area of contaminated land in the UK is approximately 10,000 hectares. This includes redundant industrial land potentially available, all things being considered, for alternative uses.

The Environmental Protection Act 1990 (EPA 1990, Section 140) required local authorities to compile registers of contaminated land and to make such registers available for public viewing. Lobbying by landowners and developers, who envisaged further erosion of property and real estate values, persuaded the DoE to abandon Section 140. This was a welcome turn of events since it was the intention that once registered as contaminated, land would remain thus classified even following remediation.

Contaminated land holdings appear in corporate statements of contingent liability and are a prominent factor in assessing lending risk.

In the November 1994 Budget, a landfill site tax was proposed as a strategy to deter the use of landfill for waste disposal and to provide a fund for site remediation. The tax has wider aims to encourage recycling and to contribute towards the long awaited reductions to employers' National Insurance contributions.

A consultative document issued in March 1995 suggested the imposition of a tax, of somewhere between 30–50%, by October 1996. For the time being, these proposals are regarded by the waste management industry as penalising conscientious operators, as a disincentive to managed landfill and an encouragement to incinerate.

Further reading

Department of the Environment *Draft guidance on determination of whether land is contaminated land under the provisions of Part IIA of the Environmental Protection Act 1990,* Department of the Environment, PO. Box 135, Bradford, West Yorkshire BD9 4HU, 1995

Herbert, S. *Remediation of contaminated land,* Institution of Chemical Engineers (ICHEME) Environmental Protection Bulletin No 036, Contaminated Land Special: ICHEME, Davis Building, 165-189 Railway Terrace, Rugby CV21 3HQ, May 1995

Smith, M. *Contaminated land: an introduction,* Institution of Chemical Engineers (ICHEME) Environmental Protection Bulletin No 036, Contaminated Land Special: ICHEME, Davis Building, 165-189 Railway Terrace, Rugby CV21 3HQ, May 1995

Water quality

Maintaining water quality is not only for public health and amenity but because clean water for domestic, industrial and agricultural use is in short supply, even in the temperate countries of the Northern Hemisphere.

Traditionally, waterways were used both for drinking water and as repositories for raw sewage. Until the link between disease and faecal contamination was discovered by the Victorians, waterborne diseases in the growing urban centres were commonplace.

The River Thames was a notorious conduit for untreated sewage, industrial wastes, animal carcasses and numerous other contaminants, giving rise not only to noxious odours but to cholera epidemics. The former, with the prevailing wind, frequently overcame the work of Parliament and the Law Courts. 1858 was the 'Year of the Great Stink'.

Diverting sewage to outfalls 10 miles below London Bridge shifted the problem from Whitehall but it was not until the 1960s that modern sewage treatment and controls on industrial discharges encouraged the re-colonisation of the river by long disappeared flora and fauna.

Apart from the National Rivers Authority (NRA) and latterly the Environment Agency (EA), guardians of the freshwater quality include some 3.0 million people in England & Wales who fish.

Table 2.4 on page 14 outlines the present concerns of water quality management in the UK.

FARADAY GIVING HIS CARD TO FATHER THAMES;

And we hope the Dirty Fellow will consult the learned Professor.

Figure 2.1 Political cartoon about Thames water pollution (*Punch*, 1858)

Controlling water pollution

Human health and amenity, domestic livestock, crops and wildlife rely upon water uncontaminated by oil, chemicals and wastes. Many uses of water do not require pristine quality. Humans and wildlife rely on unpolluted water, but it is often unnecessary to clean-up waterways used only for shipping. Classification systems for water uses are thus adopted. The aim of the Environment Agency in England and Wales is to consolidate and improve water quality. Recent reports indicate that improvement has occurred in some 11% of surface waters.

Maintaining water quality relies not only upon control of discharges and dumping but upon the siting of industry. Agricultural run-off nevertheless produces the greatest volume of excess nutrient to the river system and is less readily controlled than industrial pollutants. Appendix II lists the water pollutants of greatest concern to the UK and the European Union (EU).

The water services industry in the UK is faced with costs of up to £20 billion over the next 10 to 15 years investing in modernising sewage treatment plants and in meeting the requirements of the Urban Waste Water Treatment Directive (91/271) and the EU Bathing Water Directive (76/160). A large part of the latter costs (estimated by Department of the Environment to be £4.4 billion) will be incurred in monitoring enterovirus and meeting new standards for faecal streptococci.

Table 2.4 The fresh-water quality issues, sources of the problems and environmental and human health effects

Issue	Sources of problem	Environmental and human health impacts
Water supply and demand	Most rainfall in England and Wales falls in the hills of the West and North; most residual rainfall (water potentially available for use) falls in winter. Population and industry are concentrated in the Southeast and Midlands which have low rainfall. Also demand for water is greatest in summer.	Resources may not be able to adequately meet demand, resulting in droughts and 'hose-pipe bans'. Requires careful management as problems have occurred where over-abstraction has affected the habitats of aquatic species and those birds and animals with habitats near abstraction sites.
Organic pollution	Domestic sewage, urban run-off, industrial (trade) effluents and farm wastes.	Contamination of water from sewage introduces pathogens, responsible for some illness in the UK in spite of water treatment (e.g., cryptosporidium). Organic pollution can reduce the amount of dissolved oxygen in water available for aquatic plants and animals. Also causes increases in amounts of bacteria, fungus and algae in the water and a reduction in some plants, fish and other aquatic life in the affected areas.
Eutrophication	Eutrophication is an enrichment of waters by inorganic plant nutrients, usually nitrogen and phosphorus. Nutrient sources include sewage treatment works, untreated sewage, industrial wastes (especially from brewing, food processing and woollen industries), storm drainage and farming activities.	Causes algal blooms which reduce oxygen available in waters for other aquatic life. For humans, the problems are related to water purification, supply and consumption, reduction in aesthetic quality of waters and interference with recreational activities.
Heavy metal and organochlorine pollution	The most important heavy metals are mercury, cadmium and lead. Sources are mostly industrial effluents. Organochlorines include pesticides and polychlorinated biphenyls (PCBs). They are fat-soluble and biologically stable (persistent) so they accumulate in body fats.	Harmful to human health at levels recorded in the environment. Pollutants are persistent and accumulate in organisms. Some may biomagnify in food chains (carnivorous organisms contain greater concentrations than herbivores which contain greater concentrations than plants). Animals (especially birds, and large mammals including humans) which eat fish are most vulnerable. Organochlorines, in particular, have led to widespread declines in some top carnivores, particularly birds of prey.
Thermal pollution	Thermal pollution is heat pollution. Electricity generating plants are the main source, but other industries also cause this form of pollution.	May cause increases in natural annual water temperatures of up to 6oC. Reduces the density of water and oxygen concentrations. Life forms intolerant of heat may disappear and those that require heated water may thrive. Algal blooms are more frequent and increased temperatures may increase the vulnerability of organisms to toxins in the water. Many species of fish are able to acclimatise to the changes in temperature.
Oil pollution	Spills, urban run-off and industrial effluent.	Floating oil prevents respiration, photosynthesis or feeding. Birds and other animals coated in oil loose buoyancy and insulation. Ingestion of oil can be toxic, especially to the young. Oil may taint the taste of commercial fish, thus resulting in serious losses to fisheries.

Adapted from: Mason, C.F. *Biology of Freshwater Pollution*, Longman Scientific & Technical, Longman Group UK Ltd., Longman House, Burnt Mill, Harlow, Essex CM20 2JE, 1991, pp. 13, 48-131, 168-194, 209-218.

Mine waters

Water pollution from abandoned mines has brought about the Coalfield Communities Campaign (CCC), to lobby for a proportion of the £1.0 billion revenue from the sale of the coal industry to be directed at improving the environment in former coalfield areas.

Further reading

Mason, C.F. *Biology of Freshwater Pollution*, Essex: Longman Group UK Ltd., 1992

National Rivers Authority *Water pollution incidents in England and Wales: 1994 report*, London: The Stationery Office (formerly HMSO), 1995

National Rivers Authority *Pesticides in the aquatic environment: report of the National Rivers Authority,* London: The Stationery Office (formerly HMSO), 1995

National Rivers Authority *Contaminants entering the sea: a report on contaminant loads entering the seas around England and Wales for the years 1990-1993.* Report of the National Rivers Authority, London: The Stationery Office (formerly HMSO), 1995

Tebbutt, T.H.Y. *Principles of Water Quality Control,* Butterworth-Heinemann, 1995

Chemical spills and industrial accidents

At least 200 serious chemical incidents occur annually in OECD member countries, causing loss of life, chronic illness and environmental contamination. The most serious accidents in the UK occurred in 1986 (a road transport accident spilling lead oxide and resulting in 150 injuries) and in 1988 (the Piper Alpha oil production platform explosion in the North Sea causing 167 deaths).

An overhaul of EU legislation on major hazardous industries will broaden the classification of dangerous sites, of which some 2,000 are presently listed.

The Seveso Directive (Directive on the Classification, Packaging & Labelling of Dangerous Substances, 1967), will be brought up-to-date, to include measures for contingency planning and improved public access to data.

Conservation and biodiversity

Conservation is managing, protecting and preserving the Earth's natural resources and minimising the perturbation of natural cycles (hydrological, photosynthesis, biogeochemical and physical) and wildlife (plants and animals) by anthropogenic activities.

Biological diversity (biodiversity) characterises the natural range and function of plants and animals.

Numerical estimates of the number of living species and subspecies within the taxonomic system vary from between 5-30 million, with only 1.4 million classified. New subspecies of birds and mammals, including primates are still being discovered in the primary rain forests (for example, Brazil's golden bamboo lemur first described in 1986 and Madagascar's hairy-eared dwarf lemur in 1990).

Natural substances remedy a great variety of illnesses, from rashes to heart ailments to piles, both in modern and traditional medical practice. It is entirely reasonable to suppose that some yet undiscovered herb could provide new drugs to combat cancer, malaria and acquired immune deficiency syndrome (AIDS).

The world's vegetation cover is critical to atmospheric and hydrological function, to protecting the quality of land, air and water as well as moderating climate. The conflict between nature and the growing human population is hardly more manifest than in the continued unmanaged exploitation of the world's remaining temperate and tropical forests.

The United National Conference on Environment and Development (UNCED – the Rio Earth Summit, 1992) resulted in the drafting of a Biodiversity Convention, subsequently ratified and adopted by all participating countries.

The Convention imposes obligations on signatory countries to protect wild plant and animal species in their natural habitats, genes, populations and natural ecosystems; not to exploit natural genetic resources without recompense to their countries of origin.

In disturbed ecosystems, many opportunistic plants and organisms displace native species; introduced species can prevent endemics from thriving. The Convention aims to preserve the natural order and to control advertant or inadvertent transport of alien species. Against these strictures of course, must be offset the historic perspective in which so many species of alien plant have been transported from the New World to the old, from tropic to tropic and from tropic to temperate areas. Flowering plants, vegetables and fruits have enriched the diets and the economies of countries and continents. Important plants include cocoa, rubber, potato, tomato and mango, to name only a few: California vines were the salvation of Bordeaux and Burgundy... and so on, unmanaged except by human ingenuity.

Priorities

At the Earth Summit, the British Prime Minister John Major introduced the so-called 'Darwin Initiative', aimed at assisting developing countries draw-up inventories of their important habitats and species, as required by the Biological Diversity Convention and estimated to cost somewhere between $5-20 million. The UK Department of the Environment (DoE) then proposed tentatively to make £2-10 million available while World Conservation and Monitoring Centre (WCMC) has estimated that at least £5.0 million would be needed to commission a minimally necessary amount of original research. On the other hand, the Royal Botanic Gardens at Kew considered that fulfilling the requirements of the initiative is beyond human and financial resources. Apart from the formidable task of information gathering, the availability of trained taxonomists and systematists to analyse, interpret and validate the information is a world-wide problem.

It is the authors' view that conservation as a single theme issue directed at habitats and species for their own sake is not a valid approach. The main thrust within development agencies is to find coherent linkages between biodiversity, pollution, natural resources, development, population growth and climate change.

It would appear nevertheless, that biodiversity is becoming one of the major unifying factors of social, industrial and developmental planning. The biggest hindrance to the biodiversity programme is taxonomic, with a growing backlog of millions of species and specimens needing to be classified within a yet to be agreed international system.

In addition to Third World development, biodiversity and environmental management are also European and North American issues. Europe now has the European Environment Agency (EEA) and in the UK the unification of HMIP (Her Majesty's Inspectorate of Pollution) and the NRA (National Rivers Authority) as the Environment Agency (EA) is law. In the USA, the Environmental Protection Agency (EPA) and the US Department of Energy are strongly committed to programmes in global change data and research.

Appendix III describes the agencies involved in data collection and the study of biodiversity.

Further reading

Heywood, V.H. and Watson, R.T. (Eds.) *Global biodiversity assessment,* Cambridge: Cambridge University Press, 1995

Swanson, T.M. (Ed.) *The economics and ecology of biodiversity decline the forces driving global change,* Symposium Papers, Cambridge : Cambridge University Press, 1995

UK Biodiversity Action Plan Steering Group *Biodiversity the UK Steering Group report; volume 1 – meeting the Rio challenge,* London: The Stationery Office (formerly HMSO), 1995

UK Biodiversity Action Plan Steering Group *Biodiversity the UK Steering Group report; volume 2 – action plans,* London: The Stationery Office (formerly HMSO), 1995

Energy and transport

Reducing carbon dioxide output from electricity generation and from motor vehicle exhausts is the main strategy of the United Nations Framework Convention on Climate Change. The UK government's Rio commitment was to reduce carbon dioxide to 1990 levels by the year 2000. While it is quite plausible that major energy producers in the OECD countries will approach these levels (see the section below on Energy demand), 30% of 'greenhouse' gases, not to mention more noxious substances, come from motor vehicle exhausts (40% from power generators).

A carbon tax?

Estimated industrial emissions of carbon dioxide (CO_2) in 1990 were 7.0 billion tonnes a year and is predicted to increase to nearly 10.0 billion tonnes a year by the year 2000. Energy demand and the growth in the number of motor vehicles outside the OECD countries, in China, India, Africa and Latin America, will certainly undermine the environmental relevance of a US, European or OECD carbon tax arrangement aimed at combating the present global warming trend.

UNCSD (United Nations Commission on Sustainable Development) is proposing an international market for carbon dioxide emission permits, between Germany, the Netherlands, UK and US, based upon the United States Environmental Protection Agency's (US EPA) sulphur dioxide model (see below) to combat acid rain.

A carbon tax is based on the principle that the polluter should pay for CO_2 emissions over and above scheduled reductions agreed under the Climate Convention and permitted in national legislation. If for example, countries were in aggregate emitting 1,000 million excess tonnes of CO_2, permits could be allocated at say, US$10/tonne, among low polluters and high polluters, thus theoretically establishing a US$10 billion market. Governments would then allocate permits to polluting industries, theoretically encouraging a switch to cleaner fuels or more efficient technology. Countries and companies that then reduced emissions below permitted levels could then trade their unused excess to those needing it.

A system could be managed by a Global Environment Protection Agency, allocating emission permits to participating governments. Countries that reduce their output of CO_2 would be able to trade permits with other countries through the derivitives markets. Carbon tax is not being treated with much enthusiasm by many countries relying on fossil fuels for energy or for income: Middle East oil producers; Australia has a growing international coal market and does not support the tax although it has agreed to stabilise carbon dioxide emissions at 1990 levels, according to the terms of the Convention.

While power production and energy use may be better managed within the OECD, the demand for motor vehicles will continue to grow, not only in OECD countries, but throughout the world.

Pollution allowances

The US EPA held its third annual (March 1995) auction of sulphur dioxide pollution allowances to power generators. Each allowance, selling for under US$150, gives its holder the right to emit one tonne of SO_2. In 1994, 176,400 allowances were sold, which although accounting for a fraction of total emissions, is seen to be a more flexible and cost effective approach than regulation.

Pollution allowances are part of the US EPA's strategy to reduce SO_2 emissions by 10 million tonnes in the fifteen years, 1995 to 2010.

Further reading

Martin, D.J. and Shock, R.A.W. *Energy use and Energy Efficiency in UK Transport up to the Year 2010*, London: The Stationery Office (formerly HMSO), 1990

United Nations Environment Programme Industry and Environment (UNEPIE) *Energy Savings in the Transport Sector*, Paris: UNEPIE, 1995

Energy demand

Energy demand in the UK and other industrialised countries will most likely be a function of shifts in age distribution towards a more elderly population and a tendency towards an increasing number of smaller households.

Growth in energy demand is likely therefore to continue but it should be expected that energy conservation, a certain amount of industrial restructuring and improved technology will contain the demand curve somewhat in Europe and the US.

Moreover, low energy prices in Europe, particularly of oil, are unlikely to lead to additional energy demands beyond those generated by demographic changes.

Global energy demand is likely to grow at an average annual rate of 1.7-2.1% over the fifteen year period 1995 – 2010, which would bring energy consumption to the level of between 10.5-11.5 billion tonnes of oil equivalent with fossil fuels accounting for 90% of the total. By the year 2010, developing countries, including China and India, are expected to consume greater than one half of world energy, or more than the combined consumption of the OECD countries.

Sustainable economic growth, if it came to Europe, would be based upon increasingly efficient energy usage, conservation of non-renewable resources and the development of alternative means of electricity production and supply.

Against this scenario, coal is the most abundant fossil fuel, geographically widespread and relatively cheap. While most coal is consumed in the country of its origin there is a growing trend in international trade led by China, Colombia, Indonesia and Venezuela, providing a lower sulphur commodity than European producers. In the UK by 1995, uneconomic, over-worked pits have been closed while for the remaining pits, privatisation may prove to be a feasible economic proposition.

Primary energy, electricity, is the key growth area in developing countries and in the former Soviet Union (FSU). Countries that have the largest coal deposits – China, Russia and the Ukraine, are committed to their exploitation, in parallel with an equal commitment to nuclear power.

Natural growth and relative cost efficiency provides good prospects for the coal industry and of course, the biggest challenge to pollution control. Coal's contribution to acid rain and the 'greenhouse effect' have already been noted, while from closed pits residual acidic waste waters are polluting rivers, streams and marshland.

Scrubbing technology (fluid bed de-sulphurisation) in Western countries reduce sulphur dioxide emissions. Control of oxides of nitrogen and carbon are more costly. The prospects of Third World production of these climate modifying gases, from China, the former Soviet Union, India and Latin America are quite perplexing.

One controversial fuel is Orimulsion, a natural bitumen fuel from Venezuela burnt by PowerGen at its Richborough power station and planned to replace 4-5 million tonnes of fuel oil at National Power's Pembroke power station, 1997 – 1998.

European sales of Orimulsion, cleared for burning in England and Wales by Her Majesty's Inspectorate of Pollution (HMIP) in 1994, will, it is estimated, be some 10 million tonnes, with the UK as the biggest market. Allegations of health and environmental impacts are being made despite HMIP's clearance and claims by its distributor that emissions of carbon dioxide, nitrogen oxides and dust are less than coal. To burn Orimulsion however, requires a considerable investment in flue-gas desulphurisation.

Micro-conservation

The Department of Trade and Industry (DTI) estimates that improved energy efficiency in offices, factories and warehouses has the potential of saving 20% of energy costs, amounting to some £8.0 billion a year savings nationally on heating, hot water and lighting.

The International Energy Agency (IEA) suggests that energy demand could be reduced by a further 25% by the end of the century from increasingly efficient consumers. Friends of the Earth (FoE) have suggested that 75% of the energy consumed by domestic appliances in the UK could be saved by more efficient design, similar to US and European products.

Investment in energy efficiency is motivated less by environmental considerations than by pay back periods, which are determined by fuel costs and contracts.

Gradual reduction of atmospheric emissions in the West are being achieved, by regulation and by technological advances in energy production and energy efficiencies in manufacture and commerce. Technology to control technology is nevertheless a net energy consumer. Hence, the emphasis on the need for long term structural changes and changes in patterns of consumption.

Each decade thus far has brought a higher estimate of total recoverable reserves of fossil fuels, particularly of oil. Anxieties in the 1960s, 1970s and 1980s about imminent exhaustion all proved to be pessimistic. Even so, oil consumption relative to all other sources of energy has declined. The proportions of coal, hydroelectric, nuclear, alternatives, have all gained relative to oil.

Energy issues are linked with other environmental issues such as waste management. Landfill gases and waste incineration can offer opportunities for heat and power production and the Government's Non-Fossil Fuel Obligation (NFFO) provides a financial incentive to develop methods of generating power in this way.

Combined heat & power

In 1994, 94MW of combined heat and power plant was installed, including in the City of London, against a target of 300MW.

Coalbed methane

One of the consequences of the 1994 Coal Industry Act will be that by the year 2005, coalbed methane could account for 2-4% of UK natural gas production, subject to the approval of wellsite drilling locations by local planning authorities. It is expected that there will be nearly 50 wells producing CBM in the UK by 1997.

Nuclear fuel

Nuclear energy is a primary example of a cost effective, renewable energy source, although in the short term these advantages are still outweighed somewhat by the lower costs of fossil fuels and their derivatives and predictions that coal, gas and oil prices will remain stable in the foreseeable future. The rate of nuclear power expansion in relation to other energy sources is predicted to remain at around one third of primary energy supply over the next decade.

National and international surveillance of nuclear operations in the West as well as the technical reliability of nuclear power stations have created a future competitive source of electricity. In countries of the former Soviet Union, accidents such as Chernobyl (1986) and the continuing high potential of accidents among light-water cooled, graphite moderated reactors (LWGR) have highlighted the problems associated with lax control regimes.

Paradoxically, the future of nuclear energy in most European countries (France excepted) depends to a large extent on the success of the cleanup programme in the former Soviet Union (FSU). The enormous political and technological difficulties associated with the cleanup and disposal of high-level radioactive wastes, not only in the FSU but in the US, puts an additional brake on expanding the nuclear programme in the shorter term.

Renewable energy and biomass fuels

Energy from the sun, rivers and oceans, wind and the earth's internal heat all have the potential to generate electricity, but because of the relatively small volumes that can be generated and distributed, most alternative energy is limited to serving local needs.

Further reading

Department of Trade and Industry *Digest of United Kingdom Energy Statistics 1995*, London: The Stationery Office (formerly HMSO), 1995

Great Britain Energy Efficiency Office *A Corporate Approach to Energy and the Environment*, Good Practice Case Study No 264, Great Britain Energy Efficiency Office, 1995

Bisio, A. and Boots, S. (Eds.) *Encyclopedia of Energy Technology and the Environment*, Chichester: Wiley, 1995

Transport

Road transport accounts for the majority of passenger and freight movements in developed countries and in developing countries it is growing at unprecedented rates. Europe is the largest single market for passenger vehicles. In 1992, 40% more new cars were registered in Europe than in the US and 150% more than in Japan. By the year 2000 there will a further 20 million cars, up from 166 million in 1995. In addition, there could be as many as 21 million trucks and 600,000 buses if the rail system does not succeed in increasing market share in Europe.

China has plans for wider car ownership among its 1.2 billion inhabitants, manufactured and supplied by local industry. Vehicles contribute most to air pollution in West and East European cities and in the world's major urban centres.

There are estimated to be some 700 million vehicles in the world powered by the internal combustion engine: 450 million motor cars, 100 million trucks, lorries and buses, and at least an equal number of motor bikes and three-wheelers. Fifteen percent of the world's population presently own 75% of the vehicles. Wider ownership can only bring gridlock to many already over-congested cities in both developed and developing countries. Table 2.5 describes road traffic in Great Britain by type of vehicle.

Table 2.5 Road traffic by type of vehicle: 1990-1993, Great Britain

	1990	1991	1992	1993
Cars and taxis[2]	335.9	335.2	336.4	336.8
Motor cycles etc.	5.6	5.4	4.5	4.2
Larger buses and coaches[3]	4.6	4.8	4.6	4.6
Goods vehicles	29.1	29.0	28.3	28.3
All motor vehicles	410.8	411.6	410.4	410.2
Pedal cycles	5.3	5.2	4.7	4.5

1 Traffic (vehicle kilometres) estimates are derived from the lengths of the road.
2 Includes three wheeled cars, excludes all vans.
3 Includes all public service vehicles and works buses other than vehicles with less than 10 seats.

Source: Adapted from Department of the Environment, *Digest of Environmental Statistics: No. 17 1995*. The Stationery Office (formerly HMSO), London, 1995, p 212.

Legislation, lead-free petrol, better fuel consumption and catalytic converters have reduced emissions per vehicle of carbon dioxide, hydrocarbons and nitrogen oxides, but more and heavier vehicles and longer journeys cancel these benefits to maintain and increase urban air pollution.

Californian legislation is aiming for the Zero Emission vehicle, which would be battery driven. Until an acceptable alternative to petrol and diesel emerges, vehicles will continue to become lighter and leaner as well as more numerous.

Rail transport is a serious and viable option to the use of roads, especially since the fundamental infra-structure already exists in the majority of countries.

Germany plans to invest more in rail infrastructure than road in the next 15 years. In addition to its plans for a motor industry, China is spending US$20 billion in rail expansion in the coming decade (though probably more on roads); in the US, rail travel has climbed nearly 50 percent since 1980. Serving the railway industry can boost the economy of many countries who have traditionally built and maintained ships, including the UK and the Far East.

Inland waterways have an interesting relatively well-maintained network in many European countries and their rehabilitation could remove bulky non-urgent loads from road and rail. Construction of new waterways require modification of river systems during canal cutting and dredging; transport of fuels and hazardous substances can both extend and reduce the risk of accidents and pollution.

There has been a global increase in passengers and freight transported by air; more than double in Africa, Asia and the Pacific; in Europe, air transport increased by 40% over the period 1978-1988.

Air pollution, noise around airports, use of land for airport expansion are the principal impacts of air transport. Innovative design and restrictions on take-off and landing and permitted noise levels have generally reduced air transport impacts but the problems of atmospheric pollution (particularly the emission of nitrogen oxides) and questions of sustainability of air transport remain serious issues. Nevertheless, the Chinese Aviation Industrial Corporation predicts that the Chinese passenger aircraft fleet will add some 1,700 new aircraft to its fleet of 400 by the year 2013 and the number of airports to rise from 104 to 160.

Further reading

Cartledge, B. (Ed.) *Transport and the Environment: The Linacre Lectures, 1994-95*, Oxford: Oxford University Press, 1996

Eurostat *Road transport and the environment in the European Union*, Luxembourg: Eurostat, 1995

Institution of Highways and Transportation *Transport and the Environment: A third position paper on current policy issues*, Institution of Highways and Transportation, 1993

Royal Commission on Environmental Pollution *Transport and the Environment: The Royal Commission on Environmental Pollution Report*, Oxford: Oxford University Press, 1995

White Peter R. *Public Transport: Its Planning, Management and Operation*, London: University College London Press, 1995

The Marine environment

Coastal pollution

Coastal pollution from industrial waste, oil spills, agricultural run-off and sewage, plus the burden of sediments into river estuaries and atmospheric deposition is a universal phenomenon.

The North Sea

A principal contributor to the continued pollution of the North Sea is the UK's annual dumping of 250,000 tonnes of toxic waste and sewage sludge. Nevertheless, the total volumes of waste into the North Sea from bordering countries and estuaries have declined by an estimated 40% since 1980.

In common with other nutrient rich polluted seas, the North Sea is afflicted with red algae (phytoplankton bloom), giving rise to periodic 'red tides', depriving marine life of sunlight and oxygen.

Routine discharges of oil and other pollutants into the oceans has been reduced significantly within the last decade as a result of international and regional agreements.

The first national legislation in the UK aimed at the protection of the North Sea, the Oil in Navigable Waters Act 1922, resulted largely from pressure from the Royal Society for the Protection of Birds (RSPB). This followed accidental pollution and seabird mortality on an island in the Scilly Isles in 1907 as well as a series of other incidents involving deliberate discharge of oily wastes from oil-fired vessels and tankers. The Torrey Canyon incident, also afflicting the Scilly Isles, led to amendments to the Convention for the Prevention of Pollution of the Sea by Oil 1954, the first international agreement to restrict the discharge of persistent oils close to land.

Further reading

Clarke, R.B. *Marine Pollution*, 3rd Edition, Oxford: Clarendon, 1992

Sindermann, C.J. *Ocean Pollution: Effects on Living Resources and Humans*, London: CRC Press, 1996

van Eden, A. Marine Pollution and the Environment of the North Sea, *European Water Pollution Control* Vol 3, No 5, September 1993

Noise

By definition, noise is any unwanted sound. The effects of noise vary from annoyance to hearing loss, according to pitch and intensity, but has little or no impact on the environment. Studies suggest that animals are affected only by extremely high alien levels.

The energy requirement of even very high levels of noise is low. Noise is differentiated from other pollutants in that once the source is removed there is no residual evidence of its existence, unlike an oil or chemical spill.

The main sources of noise in the environment are transport, industrial plant, construction and ambient neighbourhood activities. Background noise has increased with increasing urbanisation where residential areas are closer to industrial installations and where a seemingly unending construction and repair of buildings and roads can drive local residents to distraction.

Motor vehicle traffic has trebled over the period 1960-1980 and is expected to double by 2020. Motorbikes, televisions and stereos, animals, children and lawnmowers have brought an increasing number of complaints to local authorities as have activities such as pop-concerts, motor racing, power boards and model aircraft.

Active noise abatement strategies are aimed at removing noise at source, with regulation of emissions from industrial installations, vehicle controls and improved equipment design. Passive measures include acoustic noise barriers, better architecture to reduce the intrusion of noise from adjacent dwellings and town planning that minimises traffic flows through residential areas.

Further reading

Chatwal, G.R. (Ed.) *Environmental Noise Pollution and its Control*, Anmol Publications, 1989

Institution of Mechanical Engineers Environmental Engineering Group (IMECHE) *Accoustic Barriers: The Engineered Solution to Road and Rail Noise Pollution*, Seminar Papers, London: IMECHE, 1990

McLaughlin, S. *Planning and Industrial Noise Pollution*, Manchester: University of Manchester Environmental Impact Assessment Centre, 1990

Nuclear radiation

Environmental pathways of radiation to human beings are well understood and well documented but much uncertainty clouds the effects of radiation at low levels of exposure.

The most obvious pathways to people are through the food web, via the transference of radionuclides from soil and water to plants and animals, or from airborne sources.

Ionising radiation is emitted during the decay of unstable isotopes (radionuclides) of uranium used in the nuclear fuel cycle. Radionuclides are unstable isotopes of any element and radioactivity is emitted mainly in the form of alpha & beta particles and gamma rays. Naturally occurring ionising radiation, that account for the background of human exposure to radiation, originate in cosmic rays and from a number of terrestrial sources such as radon and thoron.

Radioactivity is present in the natural environment and pervades the cosmos. All living tissue contains radioactive substances; energy (nuclear power) and health (X-rays, radiation therapy, radio-isotope analysis) derive their benefits from controlled use of radiation. The potential for harmful effects are derived from radiation of both natural and artificial origin but nuclear power anxieties centre upon the longevity of radionuclides in materials used in the nuclear fuel cycle, which includes the disposal of radioactive waste.

Effects of ionising radiation

The interaction of ionising radiation with body tissues, can result in cells that carry DNA abnormalities and hence a predisposition to cancer and hereditary defects. It is assumed that there is no threshold level below which cancers and hereditary effects do not occur and that there is a linear relationship between radiation received by populations and individuals and the risk of harm (see Table 2.6).

Table 2.6 Radiation doses and effects on human health

Dose (Sieverts)	Consequence	Affecting:
100	Death (population)	Central nervous system
3	Death (50% population)	Bone marrow in 1-2 months
1-3	Probable radiation injury	
>1	5% Risk of cancer per sievert	
>0.1	0.5% risk of cancer in linear relationship	
0.0028 (2.8 mSv)	Natural radiation	
0.001-0.050 (1-50 mSv)	Recommended maximum exposure limits for the public and for radiation workers	

Source: UNSCEAR, *Radiation Risks*, Geneva: United Nations Scientific Committee on the Effects of Radiation, 1989.

The calculation of the risks to individuals and populations from high and low levels of radiation (linearity) assumes a risk of one latent cancer appearing over a period of 30-40 years following 20 mSv exposure.

Lack of certainty concerning low level exposures to radiation are due mostly to difficulties in weighing social and other environmental factors, which can compound or compensate for radiation effects. Negative factors include smoking and vehicle emissions, while mitigating factors can include climate, altitude and latitude. The basic assumption of United Nations Scientific Committee on the Effects of Radiation (UNSCEAR) and others working in the field is that any increase in human exposure will result in an increase in the incidence of cancer, however small.

Nevertheless, the likely effects of radiation on the human body at higher levels (one sievert and above) are better understood than the effects of chemicals and air pollutants, food additives or pesticides since human response to radiation is measured and monitored directly. Reasonably reliable estimates of the maximum effects of various levels of radiation on the human body are available, not only from the Hiroshima and Nagasaki studies but from patients with chronic conditions exposed to medically prescribed doses, X-rays and occupational radiation.

It is evident from the levels of natural radiation to which individuals and populations are exposed that the body's natural immune system is able to withstand moderate doses of radiation from natural and man-made sources. But there is no clear correlation between illness and variations in exposure to natural radiation levels, or at levels below 100 millisieverts.

Global radiation, i.e., average exposure of the world population to industrial sources in addition to natural background radiation, is of the order of 14 million person-sieverts a year, equivalent to an average dose of 0.0028 sieverts, or 2.8 millisieverts (mSv) per person (5,000 million global population) per year.

Natural sources are cosmic and galactic gamma rays, radon gases in rocks, soils, groundwater and building materials and radioactive potassium in human tissues. UNSCEAR estimates that background levels of natural radiation exposure from all sources, revising previous estimates of radon and its daughter radionuclides, increased from 2.0 mSv in 1977 to 2.4 mSv in 1988. Average exposure to man-made sources of radiation appears to have remained at a level of approximately 0.4 mSv a year.

Radon

Radon in the home is the main source of human exposure to ionising radiation. Radon is a naturally occurring radioactive gas produced by radium decay in rocks and soils. Lack of ventilation in energy efficient or unventilated homes traps radon and increases the potential for developing lung cancer in individuals later in life from irradiation by alpha particles.

Radon is easy to detect and relatively inexpensive to reduce. In the UK, the National Radiological Protection Board has established an 'action level' of 20 mSv a year in existing homes and a design level in new homes against an existing average of 1 mSv. The US Environmental Protection Agency in a study of 20,000 homes in 17 states, found 25% to contain higher than normal radon levels (which in the US would typically average the equivalent of 7.5 mSv), which in part explains the generally higher levels of natural radiation to which US citizens are exposed. In certain European countries, background levels in existing homes range from an average of 1 mSv (0.25-250 mSv) in the UK to up to 40 mSv, in Finland, Norway and Sweden.

IRCP (the International Commission on Radiological Protection) recommends that for members of the public, annual average exposure to man-made radiation should not exceed 1 mSv, which is substantially less than the levels to which individuals and populations are normally exposed, with no more than a 50 mSv average for the most exposed workers. Although some annual variations are permissible within these limits, the annual average exposure within a lifetime for members of the public should not exceed 1 mSv. The National Radiation Protection Board however, recommends that time-averaged restriction on individual occupation exposure should be 15 mSv and 0.5 mSv from a single nuclear power station site to members of the public.

It appears that annual doses in the range of 3-8 mSv of workers in the UK nuclear industry have been typical in recent years, with an average annual dose of 2 mSv a year compared to an average of 1.1 mSv among radiation workers generally (airline workers, medical workers and miners) reflecting a continuing emphasis in the nuclear industry upon optimising radiation protection.

The point about nuclear energy is that the background risks from well designed and efficient operation can be demonstrated to be very low. While this is true for Europe and the US the same cannot confidently be said of the design and operation of reactors in Eastern Europe and the former Soviet Union.

Table 2.7 Occupational exposure to radiation: average individual doses by occupation, 1987

Occupation	Numbers employed	Collective dose (mSv)	Average individual dose (mSv)
Mining (non-coal)	2,000	28.0	14.0
Nuclear industry	50,000	92.0	2.0
Air Crew	20,000	10.0	2.0
Mining (coal)	81,500	96.0	1.2
Defence	16,900	17.0	1.0
General industry	21,000	13.0	0.6
Health	64,000	10.8	0.1
Academic	13,000	1.3	0.1
TOTAL	265,000	300.0	1.1

Source: National Radiation Protection Board.

Further reading

Barr, H.M., Cawse, P.A. and Howarth, J.M. *The Impact on the Terrestrial Environment of Radioactive Discharges from Nuclear Sites in Scotland*, Edinburgh: Scottish Office The Stationery Office (formerly HMSO), 1994

Brown, G. and Wright, J. *Physical Resources and Environment: Energy 2 – Nuclear and Alternatives*, Open University, 1995

Waste

Urbanisation, industrialisation, materials selection and use, packaging, disposal methods and constraints determine the volume and diversity of waste. Stable populations in the West are not expected to generate much larger quantities than at present, but to reduce, convert and recycle. The energy, chemical and radiological (nuclear) industries produce volumes of hazardous wastes that uncontained pose serious threats to public health and to the health of other living species.

Estimates on the quantities of domestic, industrial and agricultural wastes vary considerably, according to the definitions employed on what constitutes detritus or what constitutes re-usable material. Difficulties arise with the reluctance of chemical and process industries to release data, mostly on proprietary grounds.

'Waste' is categorised broadly as municipal (domestic and consumer), industrial (hazardous/toxic and non-hazardous), agricultural, extraction (mining, construction, etc.) and sewage sludge from domestic, agricultural and industrial sources.

Figure 2.2 estimates waste arisings in the UK.

In England and Wales, most waste is consigned to landfill. Geographical features favour this method and the British public is very much against alternative disposal routes. Public antipathy to incineration is due largely to the bad smells and the potential release of

	Percentage of total arisings
Agriculture	22.0
Mining and quarrying	25.0
Sewage sludge	9.0
Dredge spoils	8.0
Household	5.0
Commercial	4.0
Demolition and construction	9.0
Industrial	19.0

Source: Adapted from Department of the Environment, *Digest of Environmental Statistics: No. 17 1995*. The Stationery Office (formerly HMSO), London, 1995, p 117.

Figure 2.2 Percentage Annual Waste Arisings by Sector, United Kingdom

dioxins from badly run incinerators (viz. the NIMBY – Not In My Back Yard – syndrome). Sub-optimal operating temperatures and incomplete combustion of polychlorinated biphenyls (PCBs) release dioxins and other organochlorines.

Sewage sludge is treated for application as fertiliser. For the time being it is also dumped into the sea. Undifferentiated human and industrial wastes enter sewage treatment plants, giving rise to the possibility of an increase in heavy metals, particularly those that are water-soluble, migrating from soil into agricultural produce and diet.

Hazardous waste

Hazardous wastes are classified as, 'special', 'clinical' and 'radioactive'. Disposal routes include specialised landfill sites, incineration and conversion by treatment into nonhazardous substances. The disposal of hazardous wastes is becoming increasingly expensive, up to £1,200/tonne. Waste reduction, reclamation and re-use of chemicals and treatment on site are becoming more viable alternatives.

Disposal of used lubricants

In Europe, 34% of crankcase lubricants are unaccounted for in disposal. Although oil drain intervals in motor vehicles have widened markedly in recent years, the continuous increase in the number of vehicles means that the volumes of oily wastes illegally discharged into the sewage system will remain considerable.

Radioactive wastes

In the US, community reluctance to accept nuclear waste storage is not shared by the Mescalero Apache (New Mexico), who have agreed to rent tribal lands to the federal government for storing some 20,000 tonnes of spent nuclear fuel rods for the next forty years pending selection of a permanent site.

Nearer home, most of the UK's intermediate and high level wastes are stored in special tanks and vitrification facilities at British Nuclear Fuel's (BNFL) Sellafield reprocessing plant.

THORP, now fully operational, will be handling some 7,000 tonnes of high level waste over the next ten years, two-thirds of it from Japan and Europe and the remainder from British nuclear power stations. Similar processing facilities operate in France (La Hague).

Permanent storage of high level wastes is an even more fraught issue than reprocessing, with considerable local opposition to a permanent or 'temporary' burial in rock formations (rock characterisations facility) in Cumbria near Sellafield, planned by NIREX, the government nuclear waste agency. A long term waste storage facility has been established at Gorleben in Northern Germany.

Waste minimisation and recycling

Despite the requirement for substantial capital investment on new equipment, process changes and the conceptualisation of new products, waste minimisation and recycling are becoming increasingly more cost-effective as landfill, incineration and sea dumping become more expensive. Government targets on recycling municipal wastes, as illustrated in Figure 2.3, account for only 5% of total wastes.

Solid waste and effluent testing are offered by the fast growing environmental services sector. In 1993, approximately US$76.5 million were spent by US companies, expected to increase by around 6.0% in the period 1995-2000 as increasingly stringent waste regulation is imposed and costs of incineration and landfill go up.

3 REGULATION

Pollution control

The Environment Agency (EA) is a 'one-stop-shop' for industry and commerce, a single source from which guidance and advice on pollution can be obtained in England and Wales. Its aim is to provide a comprehensive approach to environmental protection and management by combining the regulation of land, air and water.

The Agency represents a merger of the former National Rivers Authority (NRA), Her Majesty's Inspectorate of Pollution (HMIP), the Waste Regulation Authorities (WRAs) and several smaller units from the Department of the Environment (DoE). The Agency has taken on the responsibilities of its precursor organisations in addition to a number of others. It has the responsibility for:

- regulating over 2000 industrial processes with the greatest polluting potential, using the best available techniques not entailing excessive cost to prevent or minimise pollution;

- advising the Environment Secretary on the Government's National Air Strategy and providing guidance to Local Authorities on their local Air Quality Management Plans;

- regulating the disposal of radioactive waste at more than 8000 sites, including nuclear sites, and keeping and use of radioactive material and the accumulation of radioactive waste at non-nuclear sites only;

- regulating the treatment and disposal of controlled waste, involving 8000 waste management sites and some 70,000 carriers so as to prevent pollution or harm to human health;

- implementing the Government's National Waste Management Strategy for England and Wales in its Waste Regulation work;

- preserving and improving the quality of rivers, estuaries and coastal waters through its pollution control powers, including 100,000 water discharge consents and regulation of more than 6000 sewage works;

- action to conserve and secure proper use of water resources, including 50,000 licensed water abstractions;

- supervising all flood defence matters, involving over 43,000 km of defence works;

- maintenance and improvement of salmon, trout, freshwater and eel fisheries, including issue of some 1,000,000 angling licences;

- conserving the water environment, including areas of outstanding natural beauty or environmental sensitivity extending to nearly 4 million hectares, and promoting its use for recreation;

- maintaining and improving non-marine navigation, including licensing of some 40,000 boats;

- regulating the management and remediation of contaminated land designated as special sites;

- providing independent and authoritative views on a wide range of environmental issues which may involve analysis and comment beyond the Agency's specific regulatory remit;

- liaison with international counterparts and Governments, particularly within the European Union, to help develop consistent environmental policies and action world wide.

Scotland has the Scottish Environment Protection Agency (SEPA), a merger of 64 predecessor organisations, including the River Purification Aurhorities (RPAs), Her Majesty's Industrial Pollution Inspectorate (HMIPI) and the waste regulation and pollution powers of the former District and Island Councils. Its duties and responsibilities are similar to those of the Environment Agency. Other powers include a duty to regulate the 'producer responsibility' proposals and powers to require creation of smoke control areas.

 # Legislation

Pollution control is managed in accordance with a body of regulation that has its genesis in the Alkali, Factories and Public Health Acts, marine legislation, Water Acts and latterly the Environmental Protection Act, 1990 (EPA 1990: see Appendix V for details of the Act and Appendix VI for a list of controlled substances). Pre-dating and parallel to European Union (Community) legislation, many UK controls have resulted from intergovernmental agreements, though national participation at the International Labour Office (ILO), the International Maritime Organization and adherence to a number of other United Nations conventions.

Environmental legislation in the UK does not follow a prescriptive regime, but is based customarily on the principle of decided what is both 'reasonable and practicable' in the circumstances (refer to the Health and Safety at Work Act, successor to the Factories Acts).

The Department of the Environment (DoE) is responsible for policy in England and Wales although several departments have specific implementing roles: the Department of Transport (roads, air, marine); the Department of Trade and Industry (DTI) controls the energy industries; the Ministry of Agriculture, Fisheries and Food (MAFF) is responsible for the economic and social aspects of farming, conservation and rural amenity.

Pollution regulation is based upon controlled releases of prescribed substances (the so-called 'licences to pollute': see FoE and Greenpeace), supervised by the statutory inspectorates, of the EA in England and Wales by SEPA in Scotland and the Environment and Heritage Service in Northern Ireland. It is a coherent system managed according to sector, process and impact of discharges and emissions on health, safety and the environment.

Until the setting up of the EA, some seven agencies could be involved in the regulation of a single company, dependent on the complexity of its operations: HMIP, NRA, HSE, Drinking Water Inspectorate (DWI), MAFF, local authorities and the WRAs.

The enforcement system

Pollution management by statutory inspection agencies relies increasingly on companies regulating themselves, self-regulation, and direct supervision by the inspectorates to reduce 'harm' to the environment and less and less upon prosecution.

Traditionally, factory inspectors have operated on an 'advise and consent' regime structured according to local conditions. Advice is a pragmatic balance of social, economic and political factors. Hence the apparent break from tradition by the NRA, which prosecuted by prescription, quite enthusiastically in the 1989-1993 period. HMIP tended to follow old-fashioned tried-and-true ways, relying on industry compliance with enforcement notices, giving due warning in lieu of prosecution. Prosecution was often regarded as a failure and last resort against recalcitrant and recidivist companies.

The UK regulation system does not rely on prescriptive methods for controlling listed substances, unlike in the USA. UK standards are set according to the nature of the process. Within a decentralised system, emissions and discharges permitted in one part of the country, may not be allowed in another, taking into account the sensitivity of the local ecology, siting of industry and the proximity of protected or sensitive areas (for example, Areas of Natural Outstanding Beauty (ANOBs) and Sites of Special Scientific Interest (SSSIs)). Decisions taken by inspectors also tend to be conditioned by the economic circumstances of the enterprise.

The new Environment Agency (EA) inevitably will introduce centralisation as intended and there may emerge a tendency towards uniform standards. On the other hand, the EA could bring about consolidation of 'advise and consent' along the lines of the HSE, with the same coherence and rationality.

Integrated Pollution Control (IPC)

IPC is a comprehensive address to industrial air, land and water pollution from prescribed installations and processes, including waste management, genetically modified organisms (GMOs), litter, etc., within a single act, the EPA 1990.

IPC was conceived with the notion of preventing pollution at source, rather than relying upon haphazard 'end-of-pipe' methods. It consolidates certain of the provisions of the Clean Air Acts, Water, Factory, Public Health Acts, for application on a 'one-stop shop' basis to scheduled industrial installations and processes. Process authorisations are issued by EA based on the operator determining the 'best practicable environmental option' (BPEO) using the 'best available techniques not entailing excessive cost' (BATNEEC).

In determining BPEO, operators consider the environmental consequences of different options. For example, capturing an emission to air might require a filter, which at the end of its life might be consigned to landfill. Is the landfill filter more or less polluting than an un-filtered emission? What other options have been considered: alternative raw materials, process changes, recovery, and so on?

BPEO is intended to be a framework within which cost, benefit, ecological and community impact, can be considered.

EA presently has direct responsibility for scheduled processes; unscheduled processes, food processing, power plant under 10mW, come under the control of local authorities.

Local authorities (LAs) prescribe air quality standards (under EPA 1990). LAs are also responsible for managing wastes and noise (under EPA 1990, Part III) and planning procedures (under the Town and Country Planning Acts).

Under IPC, the instrument of control is the licence to operate, issued as an authorisation by the EA. Without authorisation, operating a prescribed process is a criminal offence; in an industrial complex, several specific and individual authorisations would be required, for which fees are due to the Environment Agency.

Appendix VII illustrates the IPC schedule. Processes that have the most potential to harm the environment are classified as 'Part A Processes'.

European Directives refer to 'best available technology' for pollution control. IPC extends the concept into 'best available techniques not entailing excessive cost' (BATNEEC). 'Techniques' include hardware and management.

The EA guidance on the uses and application of BATNEEC is available in a series of process-related guidance notes (PGNs). However, the ultimate decision on what BATNEEC might be in particular circumstances, is a matter for determination between the company and the inspectorate. In reaching a decision, the appositeness of the guidance notes are measured against the following additional factors:

- current state of knowledge;

- financial implications (capital and revenue);

- local conditions (the process and the medium).

The IPC timetable for process authorisation is staggered over the period 1991-1996, according to process and sector, taking into account the number of processes (approx. 5,000) and companies (approx. 20,000) that need to be accommodated. Appendix VIII shows the industrial classifications of installations.

After April 1991, all new factories and process changes require authorisation from the EA and a determination as to whether control is to be exercised by the EA or the local authority.

Application for process authorisations specify the type, quantity and fate of substances discharged to water or land or emitted to the atmosphere. The EA or the local authority specifies permitted levels of discharge or emission, endorsing as appropriate the control method to be adopted (BATNEEC). The EA charges a scale of fees to process each application for process authorisation, the full rate for which is currently £3,860 (1994–95). These charges provide the basis of the EA's income and viability as a cost centre.

Environmental legislation

EPA 1990 (Appendix V) provides the framework for pollution prevention and control in the UK among the companies operating the 5,000 or so most polluting processes for which authorisation is required. Other legislation, the Water Acts, the Town & Country Planning Acts and regulations implemented by local authorities (air, waste, noise, etc.) exercise their fiat on smaller industries classified as small to medium-sized enterprises (SMEs), farmers and food process industries.

Common law is available for civil actions, property disputes and claims for damages or compensation. The most significant case law precedents have been collated in a series of 'toxic torts' described in Table 3.1.

Table 3.1 The toxic torts

Toxic tort	Description
Rylands vs Fletcher – Natural Use of Land	First established in the case of Rylands vs Fletcher, 1865 ((1865) H&C 774)). In this, the defendant had constructed a reservoir on his land. The contractors failed to block off mine shafts so that when the reservoir was filled, water entered the shafts and flooded an adjacent mine belonging to the plaintiff.
Nuisance	Nuisance in the context of land or property is 'unlawful interference with a person's use or enjoyment [of land], or of some right over, or in connection with it'. In determining what constitutes nuisance, a court would take into account the location of the nuisance in relation to the complaint, duration of exposure to the nuisance and any hyper-sensitivity on the part of the plaintiff.
Trespass	Trespass involves direct interference with personal or proprietary rights without lawful excuse. 'Interference' would be purposeful rather than incidental or accidental. For example, dumping rubbish into someone's property would be direct trespass whereas allowing tiles to fall off a badly repaired roof into your neighbour's back garden would not be.
Negligence	Negligence occurs where fault can be attributed. A litigant would claim a duty of care that had not been met and that foreseeable damage had resulted.

Source: Adapted from Ball, S. and Bell S. *Environmental Law: The Law and Policy Relating to the Protection of the Environment,* Blackstone Press Limited, 9-15 Aldine Street, London W12 8AW, 1991, pp. 133-152.

Further reading

Goethem, A.van *Environmental protection: review of European Union legislation*, Brussels: Europe Information Service, 1995

European environment law for industry: Legislation status report, Tunbridge Wells: Agra Europe (London) Ltd 1994–

Stone, C. *Environment Legislation and Business in the 90's*, Business and the Environment Practitioner Series, 100 High Street, Letchworth, Herts: Stanley Thorne (Publishers) Ltd., 1994

Smith, H. L. *Energy and Environment Regulation*, Macmillan Publishers, 1996

Dosi, C. *Nonpoint Source Pollution Regulation: Issues and Analysis*, Kluwer Academic (Publishers), 1994

Edwards, T. *Implications of Water Regulation for Industry*, Business and the Environment Practitioner Series, 100 High Street, Letchworth, Herts: Stanley Thorne (Publishers) Ltd., 1994

The European dimension

The 1957 Treaty of Rome made no provisions for community inspired environment actions, although in 1972, following the Stockholm Conference, the European Community (EC) Heads of State declared the First Environmental Action Programme. The environment undoubtedly has been the most prominent and in many respects the most transparent feature of concerted European action, even without the Single European Action (SEA), which in effect was the first legal endorsement of Europe wide environmental programmes that had been under way for the previous twenty years and more.

The SEA resulted in amendments to the Treaty of Rome requiring that action taken by the EC on the environment should be based on the principles of prevention, that environmental damage should be rectified at source as a priority, and that the polluter should pay. In addition, a 'subsidiarity principle' redefined the community role in that the European Union should intervene only where environmental objectives cannot be achieved by individual member states.

Until SEA, all community decisions had to be reached unanimously. Implementing the detailed requirements of EC Directives did not always suit the countries that would have more to pay or those with strong industrial lobbies. Directives such as 88/609 on Emissions from Large Combustion Plants (controlling emissions associated acid rain) and 85/337 on Environmental Impact Assessment were delayed for several years due to the use of national vetoes by one or two key states, including the UK.

With the Treaty on European Union (TEU – the Maastricht Treaty), most agreements are now made on 'qualified majority' voting, rather than on unanimity, with the consequence of speeding up the integration of European law into national statutes. The TEU also reaffirmed the environment as an integral part of EU policy as a specific European 'sphere of activity'.

By June 1994, the European Union had adopted 445 environmental legislative instruments, including 196 Directives, 40 Regulations, 150 Decisions and 14 Recommendations and Resolutions. Many of the principles of EPA 1990 have their roots in EU influence and Directives: IPC and the 'polluter pays principle', the most significant.

The EU is not empowered to prosecute Member States for non-compliance with Regulations or Directives. Non-compliance essentially would be failure by a Member State to enact appropriate legislation in response to these instruments. In that event, a 'Reasoned Opinion' would be delivered, admonishing the State for its negligence, accompanied by due publicity.

If the Reasoned Opinion does not cause the State to rectify the situation, the case may then go to the European Court of Justice. The Court is declaratory and it has no power to seize State assets or to otherwise to force compliance.

Citizens of the EU can bring cases to the European Court of Justice. The majority of cases thus far have been in employment, women's rights and pensioner rights under the Equal Opportunities Act. Decisions of the European Court tend to favour the plaintive, which upholds both the spirit and the letter of national legislation that derived in the first instance from EU Directive.

The Fifth Environmental Action Programme

The EU Fifth Environmental Action Programme (FEAP) runs from 1992-2000 and is entitled 'Towards Sustainability'. Its objective is to define society's role in achieving sustainable economic growth and in 'respecting the environment'; to maintain the 'polluter pays principle' and the precautionary approach to pollution prevention and control; and to promote the environment as a factor – *sine qua non* – in the policy making process.

FEAP proposes an environmental strategy that relies upon a shared principle of responsibility between central and local government, public and private sector enterprises and the public at large. Implementation pre-supposes effective legislation, fiscal and market-based incentives and penalties, better data, research (R&D) and appropriate levels of funding by government and by industry.

As with previous Action Plans, FEAP is not obligatory on Member States. It is planned as a framework in which future Community legislation can be proposed.

The European Environmental Agency (EEA)

Copenhagen is the headquarters of the EEA (1994), created by EC Regulation in 1989. The EEA will co-ordinate national environmental monitoring and research programmes, providing a centre for 'objective and reliable environmental information at the European level [to help] EC and its Member States formulate sound policies to protect the environment'.

EEA's prime function is to gather, process and harmonise European environmental data. Methods of pollution monitoring vary between countries, such that in some cases data give the impression that pollution levels sharply rise and fall at national borders!

Regular reports on air and water quality, the state of Europe's soil, fauna, flora and biotopes, natural resources, waste management and coastal protection will allow EEA to compare national and inter-industry environmental performance. It has set up national information networks and 'topic centres' to enable these comparisons to be made, assist European policy and establish national priorities.

In late 1995 the EEA will probably take on a role wider than data collection. Other functions will be:

• Setting criteria for and implementing Eco-labelling;
• Revising the Directive on environmental impact assessment;
• Monitoring the implementation of environmental legislation.

International conventions, treaties and agreements

According to the UNEP Register of International Treaties, there are approximately 140 instruments relating to health, safety and the environment (pollution control, species protection, etc.), to which the UK is party and which are embodied into appropriate UK legislation. Appendix IX lists and describes some of these conventions, treaties and agreements.

In many cases, regulations already in existence in mature industrial countries provide the basis of international agreements that seek to harmonise standards and maintain the much quoted 'level playing field' for the purposes of international trade and fair competition.

It is a difficult task for the EU to raise standards uniformly throughout the Union, especially in countries where inspection, public opinion, access to the courts and political will are less robust. EU legislation still in the 'pending' file is described in Appendix X.

Prosecutions and fines

One of the traditional barriers to improvements in health, safety and the environment is corporate reluctance to release and share accident information on circumstances, causation and consequences, or even to admit liability. Public enquiry is now an inevitable outcome of a major accident or incident, in order that evidence can be assessed independently and to allocate responsibility. Criminal or civil action can then follow.

In Europe and the US, anti-pollution regulations date from the industrial acts of the nineteenth century but levels of penalty have begun only recently to be perceived as anything of a deterrent.

Although firmly within the criminal law, offences under health, safety and environmental legislation are held to be morally neutral since they are for the most part related to industrial growth and employment. On the other hand, negligence to the point of criminality can lead to unlimited fines and prison.

Thus, the public and the Courts are still ambivalent about the concept of 'environmental crime'. A more serious view is taken of companies that flout the law for profit, which is frequently the case in matters of illicit waste disposal.

There are many effective alternative sanctions to prosecution that can be applied against companies that may be tardy in meeting statutory obligations. Measures can include:

Non-criminal sanctions:

- improvement notices

- enforcement notices

- revocation of licence or permits to operate

- modification of licences/permits

- refusal to grant licences/permits

- compliance notices

Informal sanctions:

- increased monitoring

- deadlines and targets

Where prosecution has occurred, the pattern of fines and penalties in the Magistrates' and Crown Courts have been as illustrated in the following table:

Table 3.2 Fines and penalties for pollution offences by act and prosecuting authority, 1989-1993

Act/regulation (Prosecuting authority)	Number of offences	Total fines ($£$)	Average fine ($£$)
Alkali Acts (HMIP)	4	7,800	1,950
EPA 1990 (HMIP)	1	1,650	1,650
EPA 1990 (Other agencies)	26	45,500	1,750
HASAWA (HMIP)	11	25,800	2,345
RSA/IRR (HMIP)	36	114,150	3,171
Water Acts (NRA)	1,067	2,199,010*	1,125**
Crown courts	39	1,750,800	44,892
Magistrates courts	1,145	1,792,740	1,566

*Including £1 million fine to Shell (Mersey, 1989) **Excluding Shell fine

Source: Authors' own database.

While it is always prudent to draw few conclusions from statistics, it is probably true that on balance many more trivial prosecutions have been undertaken under the Water Acts than under other instruments of environmental or other legislation.

Results of prosecution

Comparing environmental performance between industries according to number of prosecutions is quite futile since many local factors of ecology, attitudes of inspectors, courts and public need to be taken into account.

On the other hand, it would be more instructive to calculate the incidence of chemical spills in chemical plants, of oil spills in the transport industry, of sewage spills in relation to the population of sewage treatment works, as well as critical loads in geology, soils, water and the sensitivities of flora and fauna.

It is hardly relevant to state that there are more prosecutions of chemical manufacturers than there are of steel makers, or that the water industry is prosecuted more than the cosmetic industry, where processes, products and services are not comparable. It is, nevertheless, interesting to note the differences in average fines across the industries, as presented in Table 3.3.

Table 3.3 Summary of fines and penalties by principal type of incident, 1989–1993

Type of incident/activity – all media	Number of offences	Total fines (£)	Average fine (£)
Oil spills	97	1,577,000	16,257
Oil spills excluding Shell	96	577,000	6,010
Waste disposal	58	331,210	5,710
Radioactive substances	36	114,150	3,171
Chemical spills and discharges	143	447,900	3,132
Metals and metallic effluents	32	71,500	2,234
Paper process effluent	41	81,600	1,990
Sewage discharges	258	449,830	1,743
Food processing	148	204,280	1,380
Extraction/construction	134	178,380	1,331
Agricultural slurry/silage	403	266,220	660

Source: Authors' own database.

Some would argue that environmental improvement can come about only through legislation. How legislation is prosecuted, however, is another matter. The pragmatists of the old school regarded prosecution as a failure and many prosecutions have been undertaken under the Water Acts, in particular for routine discharges or accidents that have had little or transient environmental impact, such as minor oil spills. In terms of level of penalty, the prospect of liability remains a greater spectre to company accountants than fines from occasional breaches of consent, although remedial and preventive costs can be considerable.

Enforcement and compliance notices vs. prosecution

Traditionally, the implementation of health and safety and environmental legislation by the Health and Safety Executive (HSE) inspectors has relied upon the issuance of enforcement, compliance and other notices as orders to 'cease and desist' from potentially unsafe actions in order to control or prevent hazards and risks. Persistent non-compliance can result in operational shutdown and plant closure as well as in prosecution. It is argued that such a system offers effective control, reducing the risk of occurrences such as accidents, which themselves can provide a *prima facie* case for prosecution.

Acts, regulation and average fines

Analysis of prosecutions of pollution offences and the fines imposed by the courts since the NRA became an enforcement agency provides some interesting material for assessing the direct and indirect impact on individual company finance and performance. It would appear that most prosecutions result from failure to comply rather than from accidental occurrences. Nevertheless, accidents due to mechanical failure and human error still account for a significant number of incidents. Information on these latter aspects will provide useful information for risk analysis purposes.

There have been several observations concerning the relative impact on industrial performance of generally low level of fines and costs against the higher impact of bad press on public image, relationships with suppliers and with environmental lobby groups. The land-mark fine of £1.0 million against Shell for the 1989 Mersey spill (discussed in more detail later in this chapter), not only had a financial impact that reverberated throughout the industry but gave the NRA windfall credibility.

The prospect of a similar fine is somewhat remote but must always remain a possibility for offending 'deep pocket' companies. The Shell strategy to reduce the probability of similar accidents and consequential fines has been to make considerable investment into improved management practices in order to minimise human error, the root cause of most accidents.

Paying for pollution: a bargain at the price?

There used to be a notion among environmental activists, notably Greenpeace and Friends of the Earth (FoE), that private recourse to the courts would be a more effective strategy in pollution prevention and control than actions by the statutory regulatory agencies implementing the law.

Selected firms in the chemical, cement and food industries are being targeted by FoE on the basis of discharge sample results available for inspection on the public registers. Where discharge consents have been breached FoE will either urge the EA (formerly the NRA) to prosecute or if unsuccessful in this endeavour, prosecute unilaterally.

How might industry, the regulators and the courts react to this additional dimension? More importantly perhaps, what will be the effect on the freshwater environment if, as a consequence, the number of prosecutions increases?

The EA recognises that there is little evidence of a relationship between the size of penalty imposed by the courts and the severity of a pollution incident. One reason for this is that damage below ground, to aquifers for example, is less immediate, less predictable and quite unobservable to the bench. Surface pollution tends to be more dramatic in its general effect, involving frequently highly visible clean-up and remediation actions.

Thus, in 1989 Shell was fined £1.0 million at Liverpool Crown Court for polluting the Mersey Estuary with 150 tonnes of crude oil. Two years later in 1992 BP paid a £50,000 fine at Chelmsford Crown Court for spilling 2,500 gallons (10,000 litres) of kerosene into a tributary of the River Stort threatening an adjacent groundwater aquifer. In the first case clean-up cost £1.4 million and in the second £117,000.

Neither of these incidents were breaches of discharge consent but the consequences of risk taking. In Shell's case, oil escaped from a corroded and under maintained pipeline. The incident was then exacerbated by human error in the attempts to clear a blockage in the pipeline which would have allowed the flow to resume. In BP's case, the spillage was the result of commissioning a pipeline and transporting kerosene without first pressure testing the line.

Thus, there is a distinction between breaching routine consents for discharges of prescribed substances into the water environment, local ditches, streams, rivers, tributaries and canals (whether deliberate or not) and wilful, accidental or careless spillages of noxious and toxic substances, the overall effects of which are more potentially severe, both to the environment and a company's finances.

The general tendency of the NRA (now the EA) was to prosecute routine discharges in the magistrates courts (where a maximum of £20,000 per offence is available) and accidents in the Crown Courts where fines theoretically are unlimited. Given the range of fines for similar offences in both classes of court, it appears that the rationality for imposing a level of fine is grounded in a web of issues more complex even than science.

The extremes of fine under the Water Acts have ranged from £30.00 imposed by Ampthill magistrates to the £1.0 million imposed by Liverpool Crown Court, both in 1990. Neither fine has been repeated since and neither was related to the offence.

The impact of fines have become removed from shame or embarrassment to being regarded as an occupational hazard. In the public mind the concept of environmental 'crime' is quite abstruse particularly where an allegation of harm cannot be substantiated.

If society wishes to treat pollution as crime or to punish polluters as criminals in common cause then it would be hard put to decide whether to fill the prisons with farmers or company directors. The criterion for determining the severity of a pollution incident, i.e., the 'crime', will be based upon the defendant's ability to pay (viz. Shell) rather than upon health or environmental damage.

The fine visited upon Shell, a level of penalty unequalled since, might suggest that this has been the worst incident thus far recorded. Quite the contrary as silage and slurry discharged by farmers, sometimes in huge single volumes (thousands of gallons) into comparatively pristine waters, have considerably more impact on local fauna and flora than many low volume oil spills. In these cases fines have ranged from £0 – £2,000.

Nevertheless, there has been some consistency here in the manner in which the courts, particularly the Magistrates' Courts have disposed of pollution offences, treating farmers and a number of other sectors quite kindly. Similar types of incident, however, often carry dissimilar levels of penalty, according to the location of the court and the predisposition of the magistrate. The oil industry, whether in refining or transportation, is the most likely candidate for the unlimited penalties available to the Crown Courts (see Table 3.2 above).

More compelling than the plans for a unified environment agency are government moves towards deregulation and the removal of the more burdensome provisions of EPA 1990. How deregulation will affect the agenda for pollution prevention and control and the level of fines imposed by the courts can only be speculated.

Table 3.4 Average fines and penalties, 1989-1993

	1989/90	1990/91	1991/92	1992/93
All media offences	184	351	446	545
Court hearings	116	281	369	419
Average offences per hearing	1.59	1.25	1.21	1.30
Total fines (£)	1,120,680*	499,890	923,535	1,311,515
Average fine per offence (£)	656**	1,424	2,070	2,406
Average fine per hearing (£)	1,040**	1,779	2,503	3,130
Total court costs (£)	47,355**	227,888	421,835	453,758
Average court costs (£)	408**	811	1,143	1,083
Average penalty (£)	1,448**	2,590	3,646	4,213

*Including the £1 million Shell fine (Mersey, 1989) **Excluding the Shell fine
Source: Authors' own database.

Average fines for all pollution offences rose by 350% from £656 per offence in 1989/90 to just over £2,400 in the 1992/93 period with an apparent easing of court costs. Presently some 60% of fines are still below £2,500 with the average in this range standing at £959.

It will be several years before it is possible to assess the impact of EPA 1990. HMIP's first prosecution under EPA 1990 was against a Somerset sawmill for using a prescribed chemical substance without authorisation. The magistrates found the mill guilty and imposed a fine equivalent to 8.25% of the £20,000 maximum available to them and costs of £3,000.

Since the periods covered by the tables, prosecution levels have fallen quite considerably. Government policy has changed. The costs of bringing prosecutions are very high and Magistrates cannot be relied upon to take the same view as the prosecutor.

The frequency of improvement and enforcement notices is increasing considerably and average fines have also increased. Prosecutions under EPA 1990 are more likely to be in the event that firms fail to register.

Table 3.5 shows that less than 5% of all fines for environmental offences were above £10,000 in the period 1989-93.

Table 3.5 Modal levels of fines, 1989-1993

Range of fine (£)	Percentage of fines in range			
	1989/90	1990/91	1991/92	1992/93
<=501-2,500	80	94	75	60
2,501-5,000	13	4	17	21
5,001-10,000	6	<1	6	12
10,001-20,000	0	<1	1	4
20,001-100,000	0	<1	<1	3
100,001-999,999	0	<1	<1	0
1,000,000	<1	0	0	0

Source: Authors' own database.

While the maximum fines for health, safety and pollution offences have been raised to £20,000, average fines still remain somewhat lower. It cannot be claimed that the threat of the magistrates' courts was a disincentive to those determined to ignore health and safety hazards. Meeting minimum standards as required has been aided by a paternalistic factory inspectorate and industry codes of practice. Higher than minimum standards have been achieved as a result of an emerging 'safety culture', fostered by the oil, chemical and engineering industries that are the most potentially hazardous as well being the most potentially 'dirty'.

A similar culture has also attached to the environment which appears to be more sensitive to public pressure than health and safety, reflected in generally lower levels of average fine for health and safety offences.

The EA could take note of the apparent impact of the Water Acts on water quality throughout the United Kingdom. According to the 1993 NRA Annual Report, the quality of rivers and canals in 1991 was no better than in 1980, despite a decline in breached sewage discharge consents from 23% of sewage treatment works in 1986 to 6% in 1991 and total prosecutions brought by the NRA in the period numbering several hundred. That things might have been worse without the NRA would be fair comment. The majority of legal actions (some 76%) have been directed against organic waste producers from the widely dispersed agricultural, food processing and water service industries. Perhaps a more effective strategy for improved water quality should have been to focus upon the regions of concentrated industrial activity, which include all of the UK's major estuaries.

In any event, fines and costs will remain low compared to potential damages that can be awarded for amenity loss and other environmental degradation in civil actions; remedial and cleanup costs will continue to be substantially in excess of court penalties.

Liability

The Cambridge Water Company (CWC) v Eastern Counties Leather plc (ECL) battle initially delighted those concerned with environmental protection. The first ruling upheld strict liability and ECL was found liable for damages suffered by CWC as a result of ECL's polluting discharges of an organic solvent used in the tanning process which occurred in the 1960s and 1970s. These discharges contaminated a CWC borehole (used to abstract groundwater for public consumption) requiring CWC, at great expense, to find alternative sources. CWC was awarded damages of £1 million plus costs and £600,000 interest against ECL.

The House of Lords, however, later ruled for ECL, stating that the company could not have foreseen in the 1950s and 1960s that discharges would lead to significant pollution in the 1990s.

However, in the search for methods of reducing pollution, liability is still seen as an important means of recovering cleanup costs from the polluter. Personal liability is seen to be one of the most effective ways of improving corporate responsibility for the protection of the environment and safety. According to a study by consultants Arthur D Little, this move has the support of 80% of the public and most business executives.

The use of personal sanctions against directors and other company officers is still quite rare in the UK, although its use is likely to follow the trends in Canada and USA where it is used routinely. In the UK, there have been two custodial sentences for breaches of pollution control legislation.

Charges were brought against a waste disposal company after environmental health officers found that 36,000 litres of toluene was being held on an unlicensed site and that the company was in the process of siphoning it into drains. Charges were brought under the Control of Pollution Act, 1974 and the Health and Safety at Work, etc. Act 1974. One director, who pleaded guilty, was sentenced six months in prison by the Glasgow Sheriff's Court.

In the second case, the owner of a skip hire business was sentenced to three months in prison by Preston Crown Court. The sentence was imposed for contempt of court following various attempts by Lancashire County Council and Blackpool Borough Council to deal with an unlicensed waste site.

In most cases, the fines for personal criminal liability have been relatively light. The most damaging aspect for the officers involved would be publicity and a criminal record. For directors, there is also the prospect of being dis-barred from directorship. Convictions travel with the director; thus, if the director moves to a new company, the new company may be affected by the conviction.

Circumstances in which employees, directors and other officers may be personally liable

In Europe and North America, corporate and personal liability is quite clearly defined. Draft EU Directives and national regulation are exploring accountability in the context of product life-cycle, from raw material origin to final disposal: 'cradle to grave'.

Where a business is operated by a sole trader or in a partnership, the proprietors are personally liable for their actions under both criminal and civil law. However, if the business operates as a limited company, then personal liability is restricted. A company can be sued or prosecuted and, if judged liable, in certain circumstances the directors or other officers would be prosecuted individually.

The usual requirements for personal liability is that the offence was committed with the director's (or manager, secretary or other similar officer) consent or connivance or is attributable to neglect. For consent to have occurred, the director must have known that an offence would be committed and condoned it. Connivance suggests that the director both knew about the offence, turned a 'blindeye' and was thus negligent in his or her failure to prevent it. Neglectful directors are those who fail to perform any duty which they know they should perform, or ought to know they should perform.

Employees can also be held personally liable for their actions. Where an employee is acting on behalf of a company (carrying out its instructions), then the company would be liable for the offence. However, if an employee acts 'outside of the course of his/her employment', then it is the employee who may be criminally or civilly liable. Examples of employee actions which make them liable for their own results (as described in Tromans and Irvine, 1993), include:

- employees using the company's equipment for unauthorised activities;

- damage caused during horseplay at work.

Traditionally, the invocation of personal liability is rare in the UK, but is expected to increase due to the increasing potential of environmental damage and the escalating costs to rectify such damage. Penalties can range from fines of less than £5,000 for offences such as failing to give information to inspectors and breaches of duty of care relating to waste, to two years imprisonment and unlimited fines for offences of unlawful disposal of controlled wastes.

The probability of conviction under personal civil liability is less likely than for personal criminal liability. However, because the size of fines, including cleanup costs, are significantly higher than cases brought under criminal liability, it is worth bearing in mind that the possibility exists.

Further reading

Campbell, G. *Environmental Liability*, Central Law Publishing, 1995

Hay, G.M. *Civil Liability for Environmental Damage: The Implications for Industry*, Imperial College Management Reports, London: Imperial College of Science, Technolgoy & Medicine (University of London), Management School, 1994

Payne, S. (Ed.) *Commercial Environmental Law and Liability*, London: Longman, 1994

Tromans, S and G. Irvine, *Directors in the Dock: Personal Liability Under Environmental Law*, 100 High Street, Letchworth, Herts: Technical Communications (Publishing) Ltd., 1993

Environmental insurance

The insurance industry is both highly sensitive and expensive in the US where pollution and asbestos claims have led to frequent use of litigation to settle disputes over environmental matters. US legislation, especially the Comprehensive Environmental Response, Compensation and Liability Act of 1980 (CERCLA) and its amendment, the Superfund Amendment Reauthorisation Act of 1986, both of which are widely known as the Superfund Law (legislation to permit the investigation of cleanup of sites where hazardous substances have been released into the environment), is causing much grief to the US insurance industry. Due to this legislation alone, insurance companies are setting aside £180 billion in contingency funds to meet potential claims over the next 15 to 20 years. These claims are mostly due to the US government's orders against industry to clean up some 36,000 identified sites polluted by hazardous waste.

UK insurers are busy taking note of their US colleagues' experience. In the UK, the Department of the Environment (DoE) has published its preliminary thoughts on liability for contaminated land; Europe is debating new liability rules under its Green Paper on Remedying Environmental Damage; environmental liability is becoming a major concern of most businesses. UK insurers are now reviewing coverage for environmental risks and liabilities.

Insurance policies generally cover damage resulting from 'sudden and accidental' events, such that damage caused by gradual pollution must be borne by the polluter.

4 TOOLS FOR ENVIRONMENTAL MANAGEMENT

This chapter will introduce key tools available for gathering information, monitoring, evaluating and managing environmental risks and liabilities. Many of these are disciplines unto themselves. Thus, readers wishing to apply them will need to move beyond the brief descriptions given in this chapter and consult seriously the references provided in the further reading list.

Information gathering and environmental monitoring

In most cases, the potential for environmental damage is clear. For example, company discharges to sewer or to rivers are measurable. The relevant regulatory authority will advise whether or not consents or permits are required for continued discharges or at what levels.

Some problems may be less obvious. For example, it may be unclear if a material that has always been put out with the general rubbish actually requires separate and safer disposal or if fumes sent up the chimney should be controlled. The regulatory authorities will provide full advice as to what is permitted.

Monitoring can be defined as measurements made on a regular basis to ensure compliance with regulations and with standards for environmental quality. Standards may be set internally or by regulation.

Measuring samples of air, soil and water can be quite expensive, with costs upwards of £6 per sample, depending on substances being investigated. In many cases, analysis of simple (and inexpensive) parameters, such as the ph of effluent samples, can be sufficient to detect if changes have occurred that will require the sample undergo further analyses.

Regular and periodic sampling will ensure that environmental quality standards are being met, but can also detect if any process component is running inefficiently and causing greater toxicity of discharge.

Technological solutions

Technology is able to offer solutions to some of the environmental problems of today. A number of end-of-pipe solutions are commonly used to combat air pollution. For example, catalytic converters are now required to be fitted to all new cars and these devices are able to significantly reduce the emissions of key pollutants from car engines.

Similarly, scrubbing devices fitted to the chimney stacks or flues can improve the quality of emissions to air, bringing pollutant emissions to below legally acceptable levels.

There are also end-of-pipe technological solutions available to companies wishing to improve the quality of their effluent (emissions to water). For example, wastewater can be treated using a process called electrodialysis, an effective means of removing dissolved inorganics, such as nitrogen and phosphorus, from the effluent.

Process changes are important technological solutions to environmental pollution, and this realisation has spawned a new industry – the search for 'cleaner technology'. Process changes tend to prevent the formation of pollutants and/or reduce the consumption of resources. In some cases process changes which improve environmental standards can also cut costs. As reported in the book *Benefiting Business & the Environment*, Spring Grove Services Ltd found it saved £30,000 per year on its water and energy costs by changing its cleaning process. The company is a laundering firm which used up to 810 gallons of water per hour. Through changes to its machinery (for example, different valves to control water pressure and changes to its water pump) it was able to reduce water volume without sacrificing its washing standards.

Further reading

Hill, J., Marshall, I and Priddey, C. *Benefiting Business & the Environment: Case Studies of Cost Savings and New Opportunities from Environmental Initiatives.* Institute of Business Ethics, 12 Palace Street, London SW1E 5JA, 1994

Access to information

Many of the larger companies with established environmental management programmes voluntarily publish information about environmental releases in reports on environmental impact. Several of these companies are discussed in Corporate environmental reporting below (See also Appendix XI).

Company emissions data are published by the Environment Agency where these have been subject to licensing procedures. The Chemical Release Inventory (CRI) is modelled on the US's Toxic Release Inventory (TRI). Data are compiled by substance, local authority catchment area and type of industry. Unlike the TRI, the report does not cover individual companies. This data is, however, available from the CRI database for a fee.

At a higher level, policy makers also need good data. Certain environmental propositions, for example on global warming and biodiversity, are not always supported by data that can assist national programmes or lead to international agreements. But data generated by environmental management programmes could have benefits reaching beyond the factory gates. To this end, the EU is pushing for an European wide Polluting Emissions Register (PER), which would require mandatory provision of release data from all industry, including those not under IPC. The EU plans to focus on the most toxic substances which are currently not routinely monitored. These 54 substances are listed as Appendix XII.

Life cycle analysis

Life cycle analysis (LCA) is also called 'cradle to grave analysis' as it looks at the environmental impacts of a product at each stages of its 'life'. For example, in the assessment of paper products, analysis would start with the forest from which pulp is obtained. The 'grave' in this case would be the method of disposal (usually landfill). Figure 4.1 below gives a general flowchart for an environmental LCA.

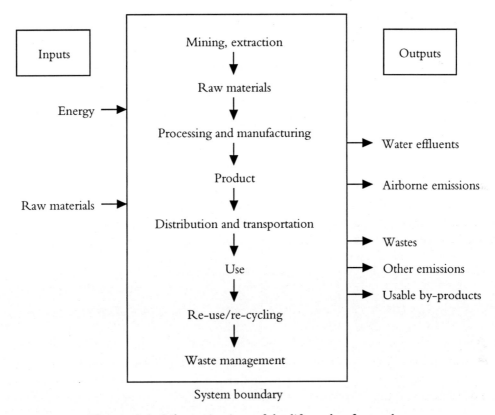

Figure 4.1 Schematic view of the life cycle of a product

Methods for conducting LCAs have not been formally agreed. Until such a time, LCA results are neither comparable nor objective. Thus, in a battle on the environmental merits of disposable (paper) nappies versus reusable (cloth) nappies, Procter and Gamble's (manufacturers of Pampers) LCA came out in favour of disposable nappies whereas the terries were found to be more environmentally friendly in the LCA conducted by the Women's Environmental Network (WEN).

Further reading

Heijungs, R. (Ed.) *Environmental Life Cycle Assessment of Products*, Leiden: Centre of Environmental Science, 1992

Viaamse Instelling voor Technologisch Onderzoek (VITO) *Life Cycle Assessment*, Stanley Thornes (Publishers) Limited, Ellenborough House, Wellington Street, Cheltenham, Glos. GL50 1YD, 1995

Risk assessment

Risk assessment is a discipline used to help make decisions where the consequences are uncertain. It comprises a range of statistical methods for estimating the probability of failure and consequential loss to a given course of action. It also enables the comparison of different courses of action.

There are three components of environmental risk: environmental hazard, control mechanisms and receptor. An environmental hazard if realised as an event or incident has the potential to degrade, directly, or indirectly, the quality of the environment in the long or short term. An example might be the risk of stored oil to seep into groundwater.

Control mechanisms to prevent such a hazard might be physical or procedural. For example, the oil may be contained in a tank (physical control) with personnel having direct responsibility for spills prevention and procedures to reduce the impacts of accidents. The receptor in this example would be the area beneath the tank and the soil structure may help or impede the transport of spilled oil into groundwater. The assessment of these factors in combination would determine the significance of an accident and the probability of its occurrence.

Each option, including 'doing nothing', presents a measurable risk, which given the appropriate data and information can be compared. In the example above, the 'do-nothing' option could lead to oil contamination of groundwater and heavy fines. An option to install a bunding structure to contain the oil could be compared to upgrading the tank and/or to do nothing if the risk appears remote.

As shown in Figure 4.2, a fault tree can be of great assistance in deciding a balance between financial and environmental risks and liabilities.

Environmental risks are very much dependent on location and are 'site specific' because of the variability of the environment. Thus, while it is potentially hazardous to store oil on a site with known aquifers nearby, the same storage facilities on another site may not require much attention.

Further reading

Brown, V. *Risks and Opportunities: Managing Environmental Conflict and Change*, London, Earthscan, 1995

Department of the Environment *A Guide to Risk Assessment and Risk Management for Environmental Protection*, London: The Stationery Office (formerly HMSO), 1995

O'Riordan, T. (Ed.) *Perceiving Environmental Risks*, London: Academic Press, 1995

Pritchard, P. *Managing Environmental Risks and Liabilities*, Technical Communications (Publishing) Limited, 100 The High Road, Letchworth, Herts, 1993

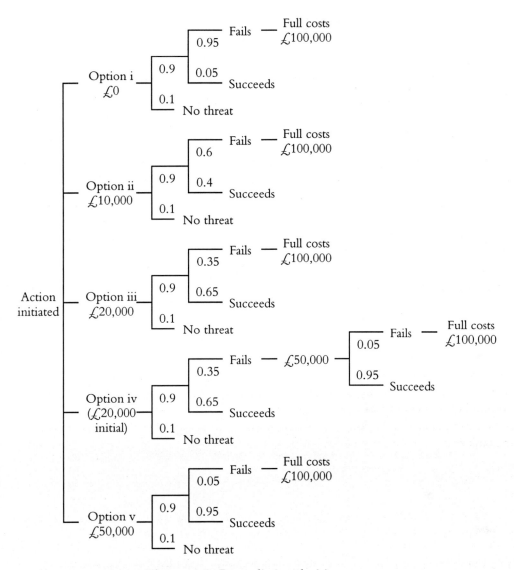

Figure 4.2 Remediation decision tree

Corporate environmental reporting

Corporate environmental reporting is a method for companies to track and communicate their environmental 'performance'. Some of the larger companies, including British Telecommunications, The Body Shop International, British Airways, British Gas, BP and Thorn EMI, produce comprehensive reports aimed at their employees, customers and shareholders (Appendix XI).

The reasons companies may produce a report are varied. For companies whose environmental impacts are widely known by the public (for example, energy producing companies and those that have been involved in high profile accidents) disclosure of environmental problems and improvement plans through a publicly accessible document is obviously preferable to highly publicised information leaks. In these cases, corporate environmental reporting has the benefit of increasing public confidence in the management of the firm.

Other companies may choose to produce reports to gain a competitive edge by increasing their standing as a 'corporate citizen'. This is especially true of large companies whose increasing profits and salaries of board members are routinely remarked upon by the media. Reporting the activities they perform for the community and on behalf of the environment is a method of letting the public know that the company meets its obligations to the community in which it operates.

Table 4.1 Minimum ingredients for corporate environmental reports

- the company's latest environmental policy statement, with dates of any reviews
- a description of the company's environmental management systems (see section below)
- an outline of management responsibilities and reporting links for environmental protection
- an account of the company's legal compliance record
- materials use and trends
- energy consumption and trends
- water consumption and trends
- environmental accidents
- major waste streams
- air emissions
- water effluents
- product impacts during use

Source: Adapted from United Nations Environment Programme Industry and Environment (UNEPIE) and Sustainability, *Company Environmental Reporting: A Measure of the progress of Business and Industry Towards Sustainable Development*, Sustainability Ltd., The Peoples Hall, 91-97 Freston Road, London W11 4BD, 1994.

For many companies, corporate reporting is a method of quality management, focusing employees attention on the environmental impacts of the company's operations.

The United Nations Environment Programme Industry and Environment group has produced a number of 'ingredients' for corporate environmental reports, which are listed in Appendix XIII. Small and medium-sized companies can produce meaningful reports on a 'shoe-string' by following the guidelines reproduced in Table 4.1 (also from the UNEP Industry and Environment group).

Formats are quite varied: some companies include the environment within their annual financial report and accounts, others produce free-standing reports while many companies produce information sheets on relevant environmental topics which, when compiled, are as extensive as any free-standing report.

Further reading

Coming Clean: Corporate Environmental Reporting Peterborough Court, 133 Fleet Street, London: Deloitte Touche Tohmatsu International, 1993

Hammond, A.L. *Environmental Indicators: A Systematic Approach to Measuring and Reporting on Environmental Policy Performance in the Context of Sustainable Development*, Washington, D.C.: World Resources Institute, 1995

UNEP and SustainAbility, *Company Environmental Reporting: A Measure of the progress of Business and Industry Towards Sustainable Development*, United Nations Environment Programme Industry and the Environment and Sustainability Ltd., 1994

Environmental management systems

There are a number of voluntary schemes which set out guidelines and principles for good environmental management. The schemes most widely discussed in Britain are those set out by the Confederation of British Industry (CBI), the EU's Eco-Management and Audit Scheme (EMAS), the British Standards Institute's (BSI) Standard for Environmental Management Systems (BS 7750) and the International Standards Organisations environmental standard ISO 14001. The features that they have in common are requirements that businesses produce:

- a policy statement that indicates the organisation's overall commitment to the continual improvement of environmental performance, including conservation and protection of natural resources, waste minimisation and pollution control;

- plans and programmes to implement policy throughout the organisation and the promotion of this among suppliers and customers;

- a means of integrating environmental plans into day-to-day operations through the development of innovative techniques and technologies to minimise environmental impact;

- systems to measure the environmental performance of the organisation against its plans and programmes – auditing and reviewing progress towards achieving the policy;

- information, education and training schemes to improve the understanding of environmental issues and publicise aspects of environmental performance.

Both the EMAS and the CBI scheme require that an environmental progress report is produced while BS7750 does not. Currently, EMAS would be confined to the following industries but other processes may be allowed to trial the system as part of pilot projects:

- Manufacturing

- Mining and quarrying

- Production of electricity, gas, steam and hot water

- Recycling, treatment, destruction of sold/liquid waste

ISO 14001 is to supercede BS7750. Both would allow companies to advertise their accreditation on their letterhead and on other material. Some of the spin-offs from setting up an environmental management system might include:

- Avoiding litigation, fines and legal costs

- Increased credibility among regulators, customers, investors, employees and insurers

- Improved cost control

- Reduced insurance premiums

- Cost-effective environmental investment

- Enhanced internal pride in company and external PR

- Improved 'peace of mind'

Some companies may find that a tailor made environmental management system more appropriate to their operations. They may choose to use the guidelines produced by the EU, CBI or BSI, but adapt them to their own needs.

Further reading

Confederation of British Industry (C.B.I.) *Setting the Standards: Environmental Management Systems*, London: C.B.I., 1995

Gilbert, M.J. *Achieving Environmental Management Standards: A Step-by-Step Guide to Meeting BS7750*, Pitman Publishing, 128 Long Acre, London WC2E 9AN, 1993

Sharratt, P. (Ed.) *Environmental Management Systems*, Rugby: Institution of Chemical Engineers, Davis Building, 165-189 Railway Terrace, Rugby CV21 3HQ, 1995

Ethical investments

Some practical questions that might be considered about ethical investments include: to what extent can they influence corporate social and political behaviour; whether investment or dis-investment on environmental criteria can persuade industry to adopt more effective pollution control techniques (or environmentally friendly processes) or to embark upon long term structural change, for example in transport and energy.

While ethical funds represent a small proportion of the total funds invested in the UK equity market, evidently, more and more people wish to be re-assured that their money is being invested in socially responsible companies.

Market capitalisation of the FT All Shares Index at the end of June 1994 was £672 billion, representing some 750 companies with 850 stocks; level of capitalisation ranged from £23 billion (BT) to the smallest at £10 million.

Dependent upon how widely or narrowly defined is 'social responsibility', there could be as much as £15 billion invested in equities, pension funds, unit trusts, building society, savings and other interest bearing accounts that have been selected against one or several green and ethical criteria.

At this level (£15 billion), the ethical/environmental share of FT All Shares equity would be somewhere in the order of 2.2%. Ethical funds under management however, are valued at between £500-750 million, or less than 0.1% of the market but it is suggested that 30-40% of investors would prefer companies to be positively screened. On these grounds, it can be conjectured that many private investors hold unmanaged stocks that satisfy ethical criteria.

A growth in the relevance of screened funds is anticipated on the grounds of widening investor interest. A large number of the classic 'dirty' industries are cleaning up, other industries are 'greening' in response to legislation and public opinion and more effective environment and safety management programmes are emerging.

It seems that one can take an ethical stance at almost any point within the socio-economic web that represents finance, the production and supply of goods and services and their consumption. For this reason it is difficult to apply other than relative values to investment criteria. On environmental issues as well, a fund manager is faced with the problem of balancing social reality with the need to take investors' firmly held principles into account. Table 4.2 describes methods of screening investments for ethical funds, while Table 4.3 is a checklist for fund managers.

Ethical investments: overseas trading and developing countries

There is frequent divergence between aims and achievements and difficulties in establishing uniform standards and practices within subsidiary companies of diversified corporations and in overseas subsidiaries where operating conditions can be difficult. At the macro level, a screened investment is the equivalent of imposing a trade embargo. It used to be conventional wisdom that a trade embargo is an ineffective blunt instrument. Yet, Nelson Mandela pleaded with Europe and the US to resume trading relations once democracy had taken a firm hold; trade sanctions against Iraq and Libya are having a salutary effect on Muamar and Saddam, influenced by politics rather than ethics.

Most Favoured Nation (MFN) status accorded recently by the Clinton administration to China is certainly an affront to investors who screen on human rights criteria; government practices frequently undermine some of the specific tenets of idealism but at the same time, the world is a highly volatile place where a morally and financially secure investment climate can just as soon be undermined by a coup, an insurrection or even a merger.

Somewhat less obvious than these examples, the employment practices, working conditions, pollution control regimes and environmental standards in the emerging markets of South America and Asia, perpetuates the dilemma of ethics versus jobs.

Appendix XIV describes the most important environmental issues in selected countries around the world, including many developing countries.

Table 4.2 Methods of screening investments for ethical funds

Screening for product	Ethical and 'green' investors disqualify certain sectors and companies on the negative balance of the health and social effects of their products or services, for example, tobacco, gambling and pornography; on humane grounds, human rights and non-essential animal testing; or on the basis of uncertainty, nuclear power. Ethical objections can be made to alcohol and armament manufacture but these would not necessarily rate disqualification on environmental grounds.
Screening for market	Ethical constraints are applied to companies that have no scruples about the markets they serve (exploitative marketing) nor about willingness to deal with despotic and corrupt regimes or fail in principle to follow correct business ethics.
Screening for social, community & employee relations	Companies that demonstrate social responsibility tend to do so across a broad spectrum of employment policies, employee welfare, health, safety and the environment and the quality and safety of their products.
Developing an environmental risk rating system	A system of classifying companies according to environmental risk rating taking into account its environmental profile and potential and contingent liabilities has been proposed.

Such a system would require unstinting cooperation and unashamed company disclosure and a vast questionnaire that would yield information at a level of detail beyond useful application. |

Table 4.3 A checklist for developing company profiles

1. The product/service	Nature of product/service (health effects/ethical)
2. Production	Raw materials (type and origin) HSE effects Testing methods (animal/vivisection) Packaging
3. Marketing	Methods (e.g., selling in unsophisticated markets: infant formula) Trading with oppressive/corrupt regimes
4. Corporate culture	Health, safety and the environment (HSE) Performance and prosecutions Employee relations (unionisation, career development) Equal opportunities (race, gender, disability) Community relations Business ethics (Cadbury Code) Disclosure of corporate environmental information

APPENDICES

APPENDIX I
The nine principles of sustainable development[*]

1   Respect and care for the community of life

Development should not be at the expense of other groups or later generations. The aim should be to share fairly the benefits and costs of resource use and environmental conservation among different communities and interest groups, among people who are poor and those who are affluent, and between this generation and those that will come after it.

While human survival depends on the use of other species, they need not and should not be used cruelly or wastefully.

2   Improve the quality of human life

The real aim of development is to improve the quality of human life, a process that enables human beings to realise their potential, build self-confidence and lead lives of dignity and fulfilment. Although people differ in the goal that they would set for development, some are virtually universal. These include a long and healthy life, education, access to the resources needed for a decent standard of living, political freedom, guaranteed human rights and freedom from violence. Development is real only if it makes our lives better in all these respects.

3   Conserve the earth's vitality

Conservation-based development needs to include deliberate action to protect the structure, functions and diversity of the world's natural systems, on which the human species utterly depends. This requires that:

1. The ecological processes that keep the planet fit for life are conserved. They shape climate, cleanse air and water, regulate water flow, recycle essential elements, create and regenerate soil, and enable ecosystems to renew themselves;

2. The biodiversity of the planet is conserved. This includes not only all species of plants, animals and other organisms, but also the range of genetic stocks within each species, and the variety of ecosystems;

3. The renewable resources are sustainable. Renewable resources include soil, wild and domesticated organisms, forests, rangelands, cultivated land, and the marine and freshwater ecosystems that support fisheries. A use is sustainable if it is within the resource's capacity for renewal.

---

[*] Adapted from World Conservation Union (IUCN), United Nations Environment Programme (UNEP) and World Wide Fund For Nature (WWF), *Caring for the Earth: A Strategy for Sustainable Living.* Gland, Switzerland, 1991.

4   Minimise the depletion of non-renewable resources

Minerals, oil, gas and coal are non-renewable. Unlike plants, fish or soil, they cannot be used sustainably. However, their 'life' can be extended, for example, by recycling, by using less of a resource to make a particular product, or by switching to renewable substitutes where possible. Widespread adoption of such practices is essential if the Earth is to sustain billions more people in the future, and give everyone a decent quality of life.

5   Keep within the Earth's carrying capacity

Precise definition is difficult, but there are finite limits to the 'carrying capacity' of the Earth's ecosystems – to the impacts that they and the biosphere as a whole can withstand without dangerous deterioration. The limits vary from region to region, and the impacts depend on how many people there are and how much food, water, energy and raw materials each uses and wastes. A few people consuming a lot can cause as much damage as a lot of people consuming a little. Policies that bring human numbers and life-styles into balance with nature's capacity must be developed alongside technologies that enhance that capacity by careful management.

6   Change personal attitudes and practices

To adopt the ethic for living sustainably, people must re-examine their values and alter their behaviour. Society must promote values that support the new ethic and discourage those that are incompatible with a sustainable way of life. Information must be disseminated through formal and informal educational systems so that the policies and actions needed for the survival and well being of the world's societies can be explained and understood.

7   Enable communities to care for their own environments

Most of the creative and productive activities of individuals or groups take place in communities. Communities and citizens' groups provide the most readily accessible means for people to take socially valuable action as well as to express their concerns. Properly mandated, empowered and informed, communities can contribute to decisions that affect them and play an indispensable part in creating a securely based sustainable society.

8   Provide a national framework for integrating development and conservation

All societies need a foundation of information and knowledge, a framework of law and institutions, and consistent economic and social policies if they are to advance in a rational way. A national programme for achieving sustainability should involve all interests, and seek to identify and prevent problems before they arise. It must be adaptive, continually redirecting its course in response to experience and to new needs. National measures should:

- treat each region as an integrated system, taking account of the interactions among land, air, water, organisms and human activities;

- recognise that each system influences and is influenced by larger and smaller systems whether ecological, economic, social or political;

- consider people as the central element in the system, evaluating the social, economic, technical and political factors that affect how they use national resources;

- relate economic policy to environmental carrying capacity;

- increase the benefits obtained from each stock of resources;

- promote technologies that use resources more efficiently;

- ensure that resource users pay the full social costs of the benefits they enjoy.

9   Create a global alliance

No nation today is self-sufficient. If global sustainability is to be achieved, a firm alliance must be established among all countries. The levels of development in the world are unequal, and the lower-income countries must be helped to develop sustainably and to protect their environments. Global and shared resources, especially the atmosphere, oceans and shared ecosystems, can be managed only on the basis of common purpose and resolve. The ethic of care applies at the international as well as the national and individual levels. All nations stand to gain from world-wide sustainability – and are threatened if it is not attained.

APPENDIX II
EC Dangerous Substances Directive – the black and grey lists

List I, the 'black list'

Contains certain substances belonging to the following families and groups of substances, selected mainly on the basis of their toxicity, persistence and bioaccumulation, with the exception of those which are biologically harmless or which are rapidly converted into substances which are biologically harmless. The aim is to stop the pollution of these chemicals:

1. organohalogen compounds and substances which may form such compounds in the aquatic environment,

2. organophosphorus compounds,

3. organotin compounds,

4. substances in respect of which it has been proved that they possess carcinogenic properties in or via the aquatic environment,

5. mercury and its compounds,

6. cadmium and its compounds,

7. persistent mineral oils and hydrocarbons of petroleum origins,

8. persistent synthetic substances which may float, remain in suspension or sink and which may interfere with any use of the waters.

List II, the 'grey list'

Contains certain individual substances and categories of substances belonging to the families and groups of substances listed below and which have a deleterious effect on the aquatic environment, which can, however, be confined to a given area and which depend on their characteristics and location of the water into which they are discharged. The aim is to reduce pollution of these chemicals, and they may be transferred to List I if in the future, the risks are deemed to be worthy of such a change.

1. The following metalloids and metals and their compounds:

zinc	selenium	tin	vanadium
copper	arsenic	barium	cobalt
nickel	antimony	beryllium	thallium
chromium	molybdenum	boron	tellurium
lead	titanium	uranium	silver

2. Biocides and their derivatives not appearing in List I.

3. Substances which have a deleterious effect on the taste and/or smell of the products for human consumption derived from the aquatic environment and compounds liable to give rise to such substances in water.

4. Persistent organic compounds, and substances which may give rise to such compounds in water, excluding those which are biologically harmless or are rapidly converted in water into harmless substances.

5. Inorganic compounds of phosphorus and elemental phosphorus.

6. Non-persistent mineral oils and hydrocarbons of petroleum origin.

7. Cyanides, fluorides.

8. Substances which have an adverse effect on the oxygen balance, particularly ammonia and nitrates.

APPENDIX III
Biodiversity and the status of environmental data

Volume of data

The volume of environmental data and related information representing the output of scientific investigation, research, field studies and field observations is huge.

More and more data are being generated in scientific research programmes aimed at elucidating 'global change' in terms of anthropogenic and natural influences on climate and biological diversity. The output of these scientific programmes bear either directly or tangentially upon practical and immediate issues such as population, development, conservation and pollution.

Public accessibility

All health, safety and environmental data are planned to be in the public domain. It is the policy of international and national agencies to disseminate results of academic and scientific research as widely as possible.

Data sources

The collection, collation and processing of 'global change' data and information has become the central aim and mission of newly established data management and co-ordination centres in several US and UK universities. In the UK, World Conservation Monitoring Centre (WCMC) is the principal international repository of data on recognised protected areas.

Biological diversity has become a central issue among policy making agencies in conservation and development, recognising the paucity of information except from a relatively small number of over-researched areas. Primary centres for these data at a 'global' level are confined to a few key institutions, in this country English Nature, the Natural History Museum and in the US the Smithsonian Institute. In addition, large volumes of original data are collected in surveys conducted by wildlife trusts, e.g., the Royal Society for the Protection of Birds (RSPB), or held in the reports of conservation societies, international development funding agencies and the research departments of institutes of higher education. WCMC aims to be the central collection and distribution agency for much of these data in order to enlarge and to consolidate its data holdings on protected areas.

Valuable sources of habitat and species data would be drawn from terrestrial and marine ecology projects carried out by scientific research institutions in their own countries and overseas. As far as can be ascertained, there is no present initiative to abstract relevant 'biodiversity' information from these data sets but much effort is put behind the development of databases of data sets in programmes organised by United Nations Environment Programme (UNEP) and national academies of science which would enable these sources to be identified and accessed.

Priorities

Data management
At international, regional and national levels, with much research already under way or planned, data priorities have been identified to serve the scientific community, policy makers and field managers. These priorities concern the centralisation of information on current research and the accessibility of data sets to provide an enlarged view of a decreasing resource.

Programmes to inventorise data sets are being undertaken in Europe by the EU, Council of Europe and others; in the USA the NASA Goddard Space Flight Center heads-up the development of a Global Change Master Directory designed to provide user data concerning global change in several discipline areas; the International Geosphere-Biosphere Programme (IGBP) is constructing a 'Database of Databases' and a similar exercise is being undertaken in the UK at Loughborough University funded by the Economic and Social Research Council (ESRC).

The ultimate utility of ecological data sets are both species and site specific. There is already a considerable volume of data that are dispersed, disparate and un-focused, urgently in need of methodologies for validation, classification, organisation, recording and retrieval. Moreover, the 'noise' factor puts a lot of data beyond the threshold of taxonomic sense. Therefore it is as well to remember that their purpose is to identify the agents of change, both natural and anthropogenic, to calculate the probability or rate of change and assess the significance of change for conservation and development planning. The elimination of noise in the system can be achieved up to a point by standardisation both of collection and presentation.

Research and primary sources of information

Major institutions and organisations engaged in research are listed below, together with their aims and objectives.

International Collaborative Research Programme on Biodiversity
The programme has set out to acquire a scientific understanding of the importance of biodiversity by identifying research priorities, developing a research programme and 'inventorying and monitoring' the world's biological diversity.

Genetic variation and response to anthropogenic disturbance, species diversity at the community and ecosystem levels and response of terrestrial and aquatic resources to the rapid pace of human use and to global environmental change are the focii of the programme.

The programme acknowledges that the world-wide dearth of trained taxonomists, particularly in tropical countries, as well as the formidable logistical difficulties of organising basic research, present major problems to acquiring essential community level data.

The programme identifies a role for WCMC to develop a biodiversity auditing system that will depend upon information accumulated in the Red Data Books on rare, threatened and endangered animal and plant species, as well as information on the conservation status of the protected areas.

Natural History Museum (NHM)

NHM is developing a data set strategy which will be derived from its own considerable volumes of species (some 6-7 million plant specimens) and habitat records. Implementation will be based upon the construction of species-backed data sets supported by Geographic Information System (GIS) software. NHM collaborates with WCMC: the most significant output thus far noted is the recently published compendium entitled Global Biodiversity.

English Nature: Joint Nature Conservation Committee (JNCC)

JNCC provides the scientific in-put to the policy arm of the UK Department of the Environment in particular concerning the classification of UK sites of national conservation importance.

In very general terms the JNCC provides a reference and resource centre for principal scientific and conservation activities in England, assisting ornithological and other naturalists' societies in monitoring habitats and species, standardising data collection methods and encouraging the efforts of volunteer field workers in data collection.

The population and distribution of birds throughout the British Isles is exceptionally well recorded and documented and accessible via a variety of electronic (including GIS) and conventional media. This of course is largely to the credit of organisations such as RSPB, British Ornithological Society and others who are able as well to implement the methodologies developed by JNCC and its predecessor, the Nature Conservancy Council.

Data management

This section of the report briefly reviews some of the international and national initiatives to centralise global change environmental data from scientific and social research programmes and projects, the output of higher educational institutes, research councils and other sources.

UNEP-Global Resource Information Database (GRID) Meta-database

This database is presently under development to catalogue UNEP
data holdings and make them publicly available. The holdings include a series of the
principal ecological databases on global vegetation, land use, 'life zones', wetlands,
climate, world boundaries, world cities population, and soils and are available as data in
the public domain.

World Conservation Monitoring Centre (WCMC)

Cartographic representation of the world's physical and biological resources is the key to
understanding natural variation and for predicting and planning for change. Strategically,
maps have more impact than text in formulating environmental policy and priorities,
especially in Third World countries where much original work still remains to be
commissioned.

WCMC's protected area database and work in this and in its map digitisation
programme is central to the accumulation and processing of species and habitat data on a
global scale as identified by international environmental and conservation bodies.

WCMC is intended to be the biodiversity 'node' of the UNEP-GRID programme.
WCMC and UNEP are jointly evaluating WCMC's data holdings to determine how
these may become a component of the UNEP-GRID Meta-Database.

Geographical Information Systems (GIS) and Remote Sensing (RS)

The more widespread adoption of GIS and utilisation of data generated by RS satellites
will become indispensable in the formulation of biodiversity data sets and the uses to
which they will be applied.

Spatial linkages are essential for both development and conservation planning, i.e.,
'sustainable development' which allows the interaction at community level between
conservation, pollution and related interests.

There is a considerable amount of material generated by RS satellite systems that are able
to enhance the development of both terrestrial and marine atlases, as products under
consideration in this report.

Satellite missions and cartography

Within the larger programme of meteorological satellite missions surveying land–ocean–
atmosphere exchanges, there is a major international cartographic initiative presently
under way to survey terrestrial ecosystems and changes in land-use, which combine
conventional cartographic techniques, GIS datasets and remote sensing satellite imagery.

Apart from a cartographic objective (UN) to map the world at 1:50,000/1:100,000,
which would be assisted by satellite imagery, there are several scientific requirements to
be met, relating to the study of the various functions of vegetation, in both the

hydrological and carbon exchange mechanisms, which are among the primary areas of the scientific study of global change.

Satellite remote sensing systems

Satellite remote sensing systems surveying terrestrial, atmospheric and marine ecosystems are the principal tools for defining the relationship between natural and anthropogenic biogeochemical fluxes to provide data for predicative models of climate and weather that will allow us to anticipate and manage the consequences of global change.

The basic applications of satellite remote sensing systems are:

- Cartography (thematic and topographical mapping)

- Global and large extent mapping

- Meteorology and oceanography

- Operational digital cartography

- Operational photographic cartography

- Resource detection (agriculture, minerals, hydrology)

The relevance of satellite imagery is in providing unique high resolution illustrations of terrestrial features (topography, vegetation, etc.) from which the changes that are taking place in land-use resulting from agricultural practices, urbanisation and industry.

Satellite imagery can be used either as a 'back-drop' for cartographic representation or directly as geo-corrected material. Typically, the area of a given location, for example representing a margin between adjacent ecosystems would be 185 km × 185 km (swathes) within a planimetric scale of 1:100,000.

The relationship of remote sensing to cartography is the near real-time global perspective that it can provide on soils, hydrology, vegetation and land-use and to meet the need to produce maps at the 1:50,000 scale on a world-wide basis for the planning of natural resource utilisation. At the present time, approximately 64% of the world has been mapped at this scale and it is estimated that to achieve 100% coverage will take a major effort over the next twenty years or so.

Vegetation inventory

There is at present no agreed unified system of vegetation classification although vegetation characteristics can be broadly defined and margins delineated. The UNESCO land-use and landcover system depicts natural ecosystems.

'Red lists' and protected species

The principles of 'Red list' classification of locally endangered species of fauna and flora are contained in the Berne Convention, endorsed in the EC Council Decision dated 1982, and in related clauses of various national legislation. The taxonomy of each country is variable according to which species are identified as being vulnerable.

The EU has established lists of protected mammals, wild and migratory birds, amphibians, reptiles, fish, molluscs, insects, athozoa and flora under the Washington & Berne conventions and the EC Directive on the Conservation of Wild Birds. For the USA reference should be made to the Fish & Wildlife Service list of Endangered & Threatened Wildlife & Plants dated January 1, 1989 and the Federal Register of February 21, 1990.

APPENDIX IV
Regulatory authorities to contact for advice

Air quality control

Contact the Environment Agency. They may refer smaller operators to their local authority.

Water Quality
Bathing waters
Freshwater
Estuary
Groundwaters
Seas
Discharge to any of the above   Contact the Environment Agency.
Discharge to sewers   Contact the water company for your area.
Drinking water quality   Contact the water company serving your area or Her Majesty's Drinking Water Inspectorate.

Waste issues

Contact the Environment Agency who may refer you to your local authority.

Land contamination/ remediation

Contact your local authority.

Energy

Contact AEA Environment and Energy office. In addition, local electricity and gas boards will provide advice on energy efficiency measures free of charge.

Environmental health concerns

Contact Environmental Health Department of your local authority.

Transport issues

Contact the Department of Transport or your local authority.

Contact addresses and telephone numbers appear in Appendix XV. However, the appendix does not include numbers for the many local authorities. These numbers are more easily obtained from local Yellow Pages directories.

APPENDIX V
Environmental Protection Act 1990*

Section	Description
Part 1 – Pollution control	– introduces Integrated Pollution Control (IPC) – companies have to apply for authorisation to carry out prescribed operations – guiding force is 'BATNEEC' (best available technology not entailing excessive costs)
Part 2 – Waste	– restructures the waste collection and disposal system, establishes Waste Regulation Authorities (WRAs), improves licensing system – creates a Duty of Care for waste
Part 3 – Statutory nuisances	– covers emissions prejudicial to health or a nuisance and powers of local authorities to abate them
Part 4 – Litter and abandoned trolleys	– local authorities given the duty to keep land and highways clear of litter, makes littering an offence
Part 5 – Amendments to the Radioactive Substances Act, 1960	– deals with radioactive substances – also enforcement powers of inspectors
Part 6 – Genetically modified organisms	– deals with assessment of risk from GMOs as well as duties regarding their import, acquisition, keeping, release and marketing
Part 7 – Nature conservation in Britain; countryside matters in Wales	– sets up the Nature Conservancy Council for England and for Scotland and the Countryside Council for Wales – describes their function as including the establishment, maintenance and management of Nature Reserves and provision of advice to the Government on the development of conservation
Part 8 – Miscellaneous	– includes power to prohibit or restrict the import or export of waste, pollution at sea, control of stray dogs and straw and stubble burning
Part 9 – Notices, Offences and the Application of the Act to the State	– a general section

* The Stationery Office (formerly HMSO) *The Environmental Protection Act 1990,* London: Her Majesty's Stationery Office, 1990.

APPENDIX VI
Prescribed substances

These substances are controlled under the Environmental Protection Act, 1990.

Schedule 4 – Releases into air
Oxides of sulphur and other sulphur compounds
Oxides of nitrogen and other nitrogen compounds
Oxides of carbon
Organic compounds and partial oxidation products
Metals, metalloids and their compounds
Asbestos (suspended particulate matter and fibres), glass fibres and mineral fibres
Halogens and their compounds
Phosphorus and their compounds and particulate matter

Schedule 5 – Releases into water – The Red list
Mercury and its compounds
Cadmium and its compounds
All isomers of hexachlorocyclohexane
All isomers of DDT
Pentachlorophenol and its compounds
Hexachlorobenzene
Hexachlorobutadiene
Aldrin
Dieldrin
Endrin
Polychlorinated biphenyls (PCBs)
Dichlorvos
1,2-Dichloroethane
Atrazine
Simazine
Tributyltin
Triphenyltin
Trilfluralin
Fenitrothion
Azinphos–methyl
Malathion
Endosulfan

Schedule 6 – Releases to land
Organic solvents
Azides
Halogens and their covalent compounds

Metal carbonyls
Organo metallic compounds
Oxidising agents
Polychlorinated dibenzofuran and any congener thereof
Polychlorinated dibenzo-p-dioxin and any other congener thereof
Polyhalogenated biphenyls, terphenyls and naphthalenes
Phosphorus
Pesticides
Alkali metals and their oxides and alkaline earth materials and their oxides

APPENDIX VII
Timetable for implementing integrated pollution control

Class number of process	Process	Comes within IPC	Application for authorisation to be submitted between	Chief Inspector's guidance note issued
	Fuel and power industry			
1.3	Combustion (>50MWth):			
	boilers and furnaces	1.4.91	1.4.91 and 30.4.91	1.4.91
1.1	Gasification	1.4.92	1.4.92 and 30.6.92	1.10.91
1.2	Carbonisation	1.4.92	1.4.92 and 30.6.92	1.10.91
1.3	Combustion (remainder)	1.4.92	1.4.92 and 30.6.92	1.10.91
1.4	Petroleum	1.4.92	1.4.92 and 30.6.92	1.10.91
	Waste disposal industry			
5.1	Incineration	1.8.92	1.8.92 and 31.10.92	1.2.92
5.2	Chemical recovery	1.8.92	1.8.92 and 31.10.92	1.2.92
5.3	Waste derived fuel	1.8.92	1.8.92 and 31.10.92	1.2.92
	Mineral industry			
3.1	Cement	1.12.92	1.12.92 and 28.2.93	1.6.92
3.2	Asbestos	1.12.93	1.12.92 and 28.2.93	1.6.92
3.3	Fibre	1.12.92	1.12.92 and 28.2.93	1.6.92
3.4	Glass	1.12.92	1.12.92 and 28.2.93	1.6.92
3.6	Ceramic	1.12.92	1.12.92 and 28.2.93	1.6.92
	Chemical industry			
4.1	Petrochemical	1.5.93	1.5.93 and 31.7.93	1.11.92
4.2	Organic	1.5.93	1.5.93 and 31.7.93	1.11.92
4.7	Chemical pesticide	1.5.93	1.5.93 and 31.7.93	1.11.92
4.8	Pharmaceutical	1.5.93	1.5.93 and 31.7.93	1.11.92
4.3	Acid manufacturing	1.11.93	1.11.93 and 31.1.94	1.5.93
4.4	Halogen	1.11.93	1.11.93 and 31.1.94	1.5.93
4.6	Chemical fertiliser	1.11.93	1.11.93 and 31.1.94	1.5.93
4.9	Bulk chemical storage	1.11.93	1.11.93 and 31.1.94	1.5.93
4.5	Inorganic chemical	1.5.94	1.5.94 and 31.7.94	1.11.93
	Metal industry			
2.1	Iron and steel	1.1.95	1.1.95 and 31.3.95	1.7.94
2.3	Smelting	1.1.95	1.1.95 and 31.3.95	1.7.94
2.2	Non-ferrous	1.5.95	1.5.95 and 31.7.95	1.11.94
	Other industry			
6.1	Paper manufacturing	1.11.95	1.11.95 and 31.1.96	1.5.95
6.2	Di-isocynate	1.11.95	1.11.95 and 31.1.96	1.5.95
6.3	Tar and bitumen	1.11.95	1.11.95 and 31.1.96	1.5.95
6.4	Uranium	1.11.95	1.11.95 and 31.1.96	1.5.95
6.5	Coating	1.11.95	1.11.95 and 31.1.96	1.5.95
6.6	Coating manufacturing	1.11.95	1.11.95 and 31.1.96	1.5.95
6.7	Timber	1.11.95	1.11.95 and 31.1.96	1.5.95
6.9	Animal and plant treatment	1.11.95	1.11.95 and 31.1.96	1.5.95

APPENDIX VIII
Classifications of industrial installations

The most polluting industrial processes are in the UK conducted at some 5,000 industrial installations. In addition, there are 8,000 sites using or storing radioactive materials. All are regulated by Her Majesty's Inspectorate of Pollution (HMIP).

Industrial installations (as defined by Article I European Community Environmental Legislation, EC/82/501)

Alkylation
Amination by ammonolysis
Carbonylation
Condensation
Dehydrogenation
Desulphurization; processing of sulphur containing compounds
Distillation
Dry distillation of coal or lignite
Esterification
Extraction
Gas installations
Halogenation and manufacture of halogens
Hydrolysis
Metals and non-metals production by wet process or electrical means
Metal manufacture
Mixing
Nitration; processing of nitrogen containing compounds
Oxidation
Pesticides
Petroleum products (distillation, refining, processing)
Pharmaceuticals
Phospherous containing compounds
Polymerisation
Power generation (coal, gas, nuclear)
Refineries
Solvation
Sulphonation
Wastes (chemical decomposition; incineration)

APPENDIX IX
International and regional conventions

VIII-1 International conventions relating to health

Convention	Place of adoption (Organisation)	Date
Convention Concerning the Use of White Lead in Painting	Geneva (ILO)	1921
Convention Concerning Protection Against Hazards of Poisoning Arising from Benzene	Geneva (ILO)	1971
Convention Concerning Prevention and Control of Occupational Hazards Caused by Carcinogenic Substances and Agents	Geneva (ILO)	1974
Convention Concerning the Protection of Workers Against Occupational Hazards in the Working Environment Due to Air Pollution, Noise and Vibration	Geneva (ILO)	1977
Convention Concerning Occupation Safety and Health and the Working Environment	Geneva (ILO)	1981
Convention Concerning Occupational Health Services	Geneva (ILO)	1985
Convention Concerning Safety of Use of Asbestos	Geneva (ILO)	1986

NOTE: ILO refers to the United Nations International Labor Organization

VIII-2 International conventions relating to atmospheric pollution

Convention	Place of adoption (Organisation)	Date
Convention on Long-Range Transboundary Air Pollution	Geneva (UN)	1979
Protocol to the 1979 Convention on Long-term Financing of the Co-operative Programme for Monitoring and Evaluation of the Long-range Transmission of Air Pollutants in Europe (EMEP)	Geneva (UN)	1984
Protocol to the 1979 Convention on the Reduction of Sulphur Emissions or their Transboundary Fluxes by at least 30%	Helsinki (UN)	1985
Convention for the Protection of the Ozone Layer	Vienna (UN)	1985
Protocol on Substances that Deplete the Ozone Layer	Montreal (UN)	1987
Protocol to the 1979 Convention Concerning the Control and Emission of Nitrogen or their Transboundary Fluxes	Sofia (UN)	1988
Convention on the Control of Trans-boundary Movements of Hazardous Wastes	Basle	1989

NOTE: UN refers to the United Nations

VIII-3 International conventions relating to the protection of the marine environment

VIII-3-i Species protection and fishing

Convention	Place of adoption (Organisation)	Date
International Convention on the Regulation of Whaling	Washington (USA)	1946
Establishment of an Inter-American Tropical Tuna Commission	Washington (USA)	1949
Agreement for the Establishment of a General Fisheries Council for the Mediterranean	Rome (FAO)	1949
Agreement Concerning Measures for the Protection of the Stocks of Deep-sea Prawns, etc.	Oslo (Norway)	1952
International Convention for the High Seas Fisheries of the North Pacific Ocean	Tokyo (INPFC)	1952
Interim Convention on the Conservation of North Pacific Fur Seals	Washington (USA)	1957
Convention on Fishing and the Conservation of the Living Resources of the High Seas	Geneva (UN)	1958
North-East Atlantic Fisheries Convention	London (UK)	1959
Convention Concerning Fishing in The Black Sea	Varna (Bulgaria)	1960
Agreement Concerning Co-operation in Marine Fishing	Warsaw (Poland)	1962
International Convention for the Conservation of Atlantic Tunas	Rio de Janeiro (FAO)	1966
Convention on the Conservation of Living Resources of the Southeast Atlantic	Rome (FAO)	1969
Convention for the Conservation of Antarctic Seals	London (UK)	1972
Convention on Fishing and Conservation of the Living Resources in the Baltic Sea and Belt	Gdansk (Poland)	1973
Convention on Future Multilateral Co-operation in the Northwest Atlantic Fisheries	Ottawa (Canada)	1978
Convention on Future Multilateral Co-operation in the North-East Atlantic Fisheries	London (UK)	1980
Convention for the Conservation of Salmon in the North Atlantic Ocean	Reykjavik (EEC)	1982
Convention For The Prevention of Marine Pollution from land-based sources	Paris	1984
Third Ministerial Conference on the North Sea	Hague	1990

NOTES: UN = United Nations
FAO = United Nations Food and Agriculture Organizations
INPFC = International North Pacific Fisheries Commission

VIII-3-ii Shipping and mining

Convention	Place of adoption (Organisation)	Date
International Convention for the Prevention of the Pollution of the Sea by Oil	London (IMO)	1954
Convention on the Continental Shelf	Geneva (UN)	1958
Convention on the High Seas (Pipelines and dumping)	Geneva (UN)	1958
Convention for the International Council for the Exploration of the Sea (ICES)	Copenhagen (Denmark)	1964
International Convention on Civil Liability for Oil Pollution Damage	Brussels (IMO)	1969
International Convention Relating to Intervention on the High Seas in Cases of Oil Pollution Casualties	Brussels (IMO)	1969
Convention Relating to Civil Liability in the Field of Maritime Carriage of Nuclear Material	Brussels (IMO)	1971
International Convention on the Establishment of an International Fund for Compensation for Oil Pollution	Brussels (IMO)	1971
Convention on the Prevention of Marine Pollution by Dumping of Wastes and Other Matter	Washington (USA)	1972
International Convention for the Prevention of Pollution from Ships	London (IMO)	1973
Protocol Relating to Intervention on the High Seas in cases of Marine Pollution by Substances other than Oil	London (IMO)	1973
Convention on Civil Liability for Oil Pollution Damage Resulting from Exploration for and Exploitation of Seabed Mineral Resources	London (UK)	1977
Protocol to the International Convention for the Prevention of Pollution from Ships	London (IMO)	1978
United Nations Convention on the Law of the Sea	Montego Bay (UN)	1982

NOTES: UN = United Nations
                  IMO = International Marine Organization

VIII-4 International conventions relating to energy

Convention	Place of adoption (Organisation)	Date
Convention on the Continental Shelf	Geneva (UN)	1958
Agreement on an International Energy Programme	Paris (OECD)	1974
Convention Concerning the Protection of Workers Against Ionizing Radiation	Geneva (ILO)	1960
Convention on Third Party Liability in the Field of Nuclear Energy	Paris (OECD)	1960
Convention Supplementary to the Paris Convention on Third Party Liability in the Field of Nuclear Energy	Brussels (Belgium)	1963
Convention on Civil Liability for Nuclear Damage	Vienna (IAEA)	1963
Treaty Banning Nuclear Tests in the Atmosphere, in Outer Space and under Water	Moscow (UK/ USA/USSR)	1963
Treaty on the Prohibition of the Emplacement of Nuclear Weapons and other Weapons of Mass Destruction on the Sea Bed, the Ocean Floor and in the Subsoil thereof	UK/USA/USSR	1971
Convention on the Physical Protection of Nuclear Material	Vienna (IAEA)	1979
South Pacific Nuclear Free Zone Treaty	Raratonga (SPBEC)	1985
Convention on Early Notification of a Nuclear Accident	Vienna (IAEA)	1986
Convention on Assistance in the Case of a Nuclear Accident or Radiological Emergency	Vienna (IAEA)	1986
Joint Protocol Relating to the Vienna and Paris conventions to avoid conflicts in their application	Vienna (IAEA)	1988

NOTES: UN = United Nations
ILO = UN International Labor Organization
IAEA = International Atomic Energy Authority
OECD = Organization for Economic Co-operation and Development
SPBEC = South Pacific Bureau For Economic Co-operation

In addition, there are two Nuclear (Euratom) Directives
New Basic Standards for the Health Protection of the General Public and Workers against the Dangers of Ionising Radiation (80/836/Euratom) of 15 July 1980 and amended 5 October 1984 (84/467/Euratom).

Laying Down Basic Measures for the Protection of Persons Undergoing Medical Examination or Treatment (84/466/Euratom) of 3 September 1984.

VIII-5 International conventions relating to nature conservation and species protection (see also Marine VIII-3-i)

Convention	Place of adoption (Organisation)	Date
International Convention for the Protection of Birds	Paris (France)	1950
Convention on Wetlands of International Importance Especially as Waterfowl Habitat (also, 1982 Protocol)	Ramsar (UNESCO)	1971
Convention Concerning the Protection of the World Cultural and Natural Heritage (World Heritage sites)	Paris (UNESCO)	1972
Convention on International Trade in Endangered Species of Wild Flora and Fauna (CITES Convention)	Washington (Switzerland)	1973
Convention on the Conservation of Migratory Species of Wild Animals	Bonn (Germany)	1979
Protocol to Amend the RAMSAR Convention	Paris (UNESCO)	1982

NOTE: UNESCO = United Nations Educational, Scientific and Cultural Organization

VIII-6 European conventions relating to nature conservation and species protection (See also Marine VIII-3-i and International Conventions VIII-5)

Convention	Place of adoption (Organisation)	Date
European Convention for the Protection of Animals During International Transport	Paris (COE)	1968
Benelux Convention on the Hunting and Protection of Birds	Brussels (BEU)	1970
Convention on the Protection of the Environment between Denmark, Finland, Norway and Sweden	Stockholm	1974
Convention on the Conservation of European Wildlife and Natural Habitats	Berne (COE)	1979
Benelux Convention on Nature Conservation and Landscape Protection	Brussels (BEU)	1982
Agreement for Co-operation in Dealing with Pollution of the North Sea by Oil	Bonn	1969
Agreement for Co-operation in Dealing with the Pollution of the North Sea by Oil and Other Harmful Substances	Bonn	1983
Convention on the Protection of the Marine Environment of the Baltic Sea Area	Helsinki	1974
Convention for Prevention of Marine Pollution by Dumping from Ships and Aircraft (North Atlantic and Arctic Oceans)	Oslo	1972
Convention on the Prevention of Marine Pollution from Land-based Sources (North Atlantic and Arctic Oceans)	Paris	1974

NOTES: COE Council of Europe
BEU Benelux Economic Union

VIII-7 International and regional programmes relating to chemicals
Chemical conventions relate to the transport of hazardous substances, dumping and resultant marine pollution but not to their manufacture or commercial distribution.

International and regional programmes:

* FAO/UNDP/ENEP Intergrated Pest Management (IPM)

* FAO/WHO/UNEP Panel of Experts on Environmental Management of Pest Control

* UNEP International Register of Potentially Toxic Chemicals (IRPTC)

* WHO/ILO/UNEP International Programme for Chemical Safety (IPCS)

* European Inventory of Existing Commercial Chemical Substances (EINECS)

Regional inter-governmental co-operation:

* Nordic Council of Ministers (Denmark, Finland, Iceland, Norway and Sweden)

* Council of Europe

* Commission of the European Communities

NOTES: FAO = United Nations Food and Agriculture Organization
UNEP = United Nations Environment Programme
UNDP = United Nations Development Programme
WHO = World Health Organization
ILO = United Nations International Labor Organization

APPENDIX X
Proposed EU legislation (as at December 1994)

Virtually all of UK environmental legislation is now driven by EU legislation. Proposed EU legislation is a good indication of the changes that can be expected in the UK.

1. The Proposed Landfill Directive

Objectives:
- to raise standards in landfill practice to a uniform level throughout the Community
- to prevent the emergence of contaminated sites throughout the Community
- to harmonise standards to ensure an equal level of environmental protection within the Community and to prevent any distortion of free competition of waste disposal in the internal market
- to reduce the need for landfilling of waste by the promotion of waste minimisation and recycling
- to ensure that the price charged for the disposal of waste takes into account all the costs involved in setting up operations and after-care facilities.

Requirements:
- permitting requirements will be based on technical criteria in relation to three types of landfill site: i) landfill for hazardous waste; ii) landfill for municipal and non-hazardous wastes and for other compatible wastes iii) landfill for inert waste
  before receiving a permit, operators will have to provide a financial guarantee that they will be able to cover the estimated costs of closure and after-care operations related to the site
- operators will have to contribute to an after-care fund
- operators will be liable under the proposed Directive in civil law for the damage and impairment of the environment caused by the landfilled waste, irrespective of fault on their part.

Implications:
- will significantly increase the cost of disposal to landfill
- stimulate development of other waste management techniques including incineration, waste treatment, recycling and reuse
- should encourage manufacturers to re-appraise production methods to reduce their waste streams or find ways of recycling by-products and to look at other means of disposal such as incineration or chemical treatment.

2. Proposed Directive on the Incineration of Hazardous Waste

Objectives: – to stipulate design, operating and emission standards which would apply to new, and eventually existing, hazardous waste incinerators in Member States

     – to exclude certain types of waste from the scope of this Directive:
  i) municipal wastes;
  ii) combustible liquid waste including waste oils depending on their poly aromatic hydrocarbon (PAH) content, calorific value and emissions.

Requirements: – administrative permitting requirements will be affected

     – stipulated detailed hardware requirements and maximum exhaust gas emission limit values for dust, organic carbon, hydrogen chloride, hydrogen fluoride, sulphur dioxide and a range of metals and their compound

     – a guide value for a range of dioxin and furan emissions to be set at 0.1ng/m^3

     – sets requirements for continuous measurement requirement.

Implications: – to affect authorisations for waste incinerators through Integrated Pollution Control.

3. Proposed Directive on Packaging and Packaging Waste

Objectives: – covers all packaging placed on the market in the Community and all packaging waste, whether it is used or released at industrial, commercial, office, shop, service or household level, regardless of the materials used and whether it contains primary, secondary or tertiary packaging

     – may exclude 'small packs', primary packaging for pharmaceutical products

     – to ensure that within 10 years of its adoption, 90% of all packaging waste would be removed from the waste stream and recovered through reuse, recycling, composting, or regenerated by chemical action or incineration to produce energy. A hierarchy of (in descending order) prevention, reuse, recycling, incineration with energy recovery, incineration without energy recovery and disposal by way of landfill may be proposed

     – final 10% of packaging waste would be limited to the residues of the collection and sorting activities

     – ban on the use of packaging materials containing halogenated compounds, chlorinated components or chlorinated bleaching agent, may include PVCs and many plastics

     – fixed maximum levels for use of copper, nickel and zinc used in packaging.

Implications: – major for the packaging industry

     – likely to increase the costs for all purchasers of supplies.

4. Proposed Directive on the Disposal of Polychlorinated Biphenyls (PCBs) and Polychlorinated Terphenyls (PCTs)

Objectives: – to harmonise laws on the controlled disposal of PCBs and equipment or objects contaminated by PCBs in order to reduce and prevent pollution.

Requirements: – would be a national licensing system for PCB disposal, licensing only granted to those meeting the technical criteria
  – operators would bear civil liability for any environmental damage caused by the disposal installation, irrespective of any fault on their part and must take out the necessary insurance
  – must ensure that PCBs are replaced by other fluids only if the replacement fluids entail less or no risks
  – must implement programmes for general public and members of emergency services on the hazards of PCBs to human health and the environment and on the precautions to be taken to ensure protection
  – must draw up plans for the disposal and PCBs and the collection of capacitors containing less than 7 dm^3 of PCBs or equipment containing such capacitors.

Implications: – companies using PCBs will have to devise programmes for their disposal and timetables for their replacement.

5. Proposed Directive on the Control of Volatile Organic Compounds (VOCs) Resulting from the Storage of Petrol

Objectives: – to improve air quality in the Community by bringing about a reduction in anthropogenic VOC emissions
  – reduction of the evaporative emissions of VOCs from the storage of petrol and its distribution from terminals to service stations as this is the source of 5% of the EU's VOC emissions
  – to bring about a reduction by 90% from this source over a period of 10 years.

Requirements: – stipulates design and operational requirements for storage installation, but Member States can use other technical measures if they demonstrate their effectiveness
  – will apply to all new, and eventually existing, installations
  – stipulates technical requirements for loading and unloading facilities and for mobile containers
  – would exempt small service stations with a throughput of less than 100m^3 per year.

6. Draft Directive on Integrated Pollution Prevention and Control

Objectives: – aims to ensure pollution control from large industrial plant to water, air and land.

Requirements: – prescribed plants would have to apply for authorisation permits from the competent authority
  – control using best available technology (BAT) but costs are also to be taken into account.

Implications: – is very similar to the control system in the UK, under the Environmental Protection Act, 1990.

7.   Proposed Regulation on Ozone-Depleting Substances

Objectives: − to extend the scope of current EU Regulations which apply only to production and consumption of ozone depleting substances
    − would apply to production, importation, exportation, supply, use and/or recovery of chlorofluorocarbons (CFCs), halons, carbon tetrachloride, 1,1,1-trichloroethane, methyl bromide, hydrobromofluorcarbons (HBFCs) and hydrochlorofluorocarbons (HCFCs).

Requirements: − would introduce phase out schedules for the production and supply of some of the substances as follows:
    CFCs − 1 January 1994, except for Member States where less than 15,000 tonnes of CFCs were produced in 1986, for which the date would be 1 January 1996. Earlier date would apply to fully halogenated CFCs and supply of all CFCs in all Member States.
    Halons − 1 January 1994
    Carbon tetrachloride − 1 January 1995
    1,1,1-Trichloroethane − 1 January 1996
    HBFCs − 1 January 1996
    HCFCs − 1 January 2015 (not including production)
    − there would be numerous other restrictions on HCFC use.

8.   Draft Solvent Directive

Objectives: − establishes measures to limit the emissions of organic compounds from a number of processes including:
    − printing processes
    − surface cleaning
    − coating processes
    − dry cleaning
    − wood treatment
    − manufacture of coating varnishes, inks and adhesives
    − manufacture of rubber and rubber products.

Requirements: − may only allow operation of new installation, and eventually existing installations, where the requirements of Directive are met
    − must ensure that operators of the new installations, and eventually existing installations, produce annual solvent management plans and that the most harmful solvents are replaced by less harmful ones with the shortest delay possible
    − sets monitoring requirements and promotes use of best available technology (BAT).

9. Proposed Carbon/Energy Tax

Objectives: — to use market to reduce carbon dioxide emissions.

Requirements: — pay for emissions by tax.

Implications: — EU ministers failed to agree on a uniform carbon/energy tax.
Britain, in particular, has held out strongly against the idea of such a
tax, arguing that it would be distortive and inapplicable in any case
given the varying levels of carbon dioxide emission in the
Community.

10. Proposed Directive on Civil Liability for Damage Caused by Waste

Objectives: — create primary civil liability for damage and impairment of the
environment caused by waste generated in the course of an
occupational activity on the producer of the waste irrespective of
fault on their part
— 'damage' is that resulting from death or physical injury or damage to
property
— 'impairment of the environment' means any significant physical,
chemical or biological deterioration of the environment, not
including property damage.

Implications: — has temporarily been put on hold pending the outcome of the wider
discussion on environmental liability initiated by the issuance of a
Green Paper on remedying environmental damage (see below).

11. Miscellaneous Proposed Waste Directives

Objectives: — to increase civil liability for damage caused by waste (e.g., the
proposed Directives on Landfill and PCBs.

12. EC Green Paper on Remedying Environmental Damage

Objectives: — is concerned with remedies in respect of environmental damage
generally, rather than damage caused only by waste
— suggests a system of civil liability which adopts the 'polluter pays'
principle
— envisages a two-tier system of enforcement, based partly on strict
liability and partly on a compensation regime when no liable party
can be found.

APPENDIX XI
List of UK companies producing corporate environmental performance reports*

COMPANY	SECTOR
Anglian Water	Water utility
Argos	Consumer goods
Arjo Wiggins Fine Papers Ltd	Paper
Blue Circle industries plc	Cement manufacture
B&Q	Consumer goods
The Body Shop International	Consumer goods
British Airways	Transport
BAA Heathrow	Transport
British Gas	Oil and gas
British Nuclear Fuels	Energy utility
BP Chemicals	Chemicals
British Petroleum	Oil and gas
British Telecommunications plc	Telecoms
Cable and Wireless	Telecoms
Cadbury Schweppes	Food
Caird Group	Waste
Courtaulds	Textiles
DHL International	Transport
DHL (UK) Ltd	Transport
East Midlands Electricity	Energy utility
The Environment Council	NGO
Glaxo Wellcome	Pharmaceuticals
IBM	IT
ICI	Chemicals
James River	Paper
Lloyds TSB	Banking
3M	Consumer goods
Manweb	Energy utility
Midlands Electricity	Energy utility
Mobil	Oil and gas
National Power	Energy utility
National Westminster Bank	Banking
Northumbrian Water Group plc	Water utility
Norsk Hydro	Metals/chemicals
PowerGen	Electricity utility
Procter and Gamble Ltd	Consumer goods
Rank Zerox	Consumer goods
Reckitt & Colman	Consumer goods
Scottish Nuclear	Energy utility

Seeboard	Consumer goods
Severn Trent plc	Water utilitiy
Shanks and McEwan	Waste
SmithKline Beecham	Pharmaceuticals
Sun Alliance	Insurance
Thames Water plc	Water utility
Thorn-EMI	Consumer goods
Vodafone	Telecoms
Wessex Water	Water utility
Woking Borough Council	Local authority
Yorkshire Electricity	Electricity utility

* Roger Adams, Chartered Association of Certified Accounts (ACCA), Personal Communication, June 1995 and 'Could Try Harder', *Financial Times*, April 17 1996 p24.

APPENDIX XII – Substances likely to be included in the proposed EU-wide Polluting Emissions Register (PER)*

The Commission has devised two lists of potential substances for mandatory monitoring and publication via the PER. The lists were based on the USA's experience of their Toxic Release Inventory (TRI).

Substances whose emissions exceed 500 tonnes per year in the USA

Acetonitrile
Acrylamide
Acrylonitrile
Ammonia
Arsenic compounds
Asbestos
Benzene
1,3-butadiene
Cadmium compounds
Carbon disulphide
Carbon tetrachloride
Chlorine
Chlorophenols
Chromium compounds
Copper compounds
Cresol (mixed isomers)
Cyanide compounds

2,4-dinitrotoluene
Ethylene oxide
Formaldehyde
Hexachlorobenzene
Hydrogen cyanide
Hydrogen fluoride
Lead compounds
2-methoxyethanol
Methyl bromide
Nickel compounds
Nitrobenzene
Pentachlorophenol
White phosphorous
Polychlorinated biphenyls
Propylene oxide
Vinyl chloride
Zinc compounds

Substances whose emissions exceed 50 tonnes per year in the USA

Acrolein
Arsenic
3,3-dichlorobenzidine
4,6-dinitro-o-cresol
2,4-dinitrophenol
Propane sultone
Selenium
Selenium coumpounds
1,1,2,2-tetrachloroethane

Epichlorohydrin
Heptachlor
4,4-methylenedianiline
2-nitropropane
White/yellow phosphorous
Toluene-2,4-diisocyanate
Toluene 2,6-diisocyanate
o-toluidene
Urethane

---

* 'Update on EC emissions register' *The ENDS Report* Number 236 pp 34-35 (Sep 1994).

APPENDIX XIII
The 50 Reporting Ingredients as developed by UNEP Industry and Environment with SustainAbility*

Note: UNEP = United Nations Environment Programme

I.   MANAGEMENT AND SYSTEM
1.   CEO Statement
2.   Environmental policy
3.   Environmental management system
4.   Management responsibility
5.   Environmental auditing
6.   Goals and targets
7.   Legal compliance
8.   Research and development
9.   Programmes and initiatives
10. Awards
11. Verification
12. Reporting policy
13. Corporate context

2.   INPUT/OUTPUT INVENTORY
Inputs
14. Material use
15. Energy consumption
16. Water consumption

Process Management
17. Health and Safety
18. EIAs and risk management
19. Accidents and emergency response
10. Land contamination and remediation
21. Habitats

Outputs
22. Wastes
23. Air emissions
24. Water effluents
25. Noise and odours
26. Transportation

---

* Adapted from United Nations Environment Programme Industry and Environment (UNEPIE) and Sustainability Ltd., Appendix 5, *Company Environmental Reporting: A Measure of the Progress of Business and Industry Towards Sustainable Development*, SustainAbility Ltd., The Peoples Hall, 91-97 Freston Road, London W11 4BD, 1994.

Products
27. Life cycle design
28. Packaging
29. Product impacts
30. Product stewardship

3. FINANCE
31. Environmental spending
32. Liabilities
33. Economic instruments
34. Environmental cost accounting
35. Benefits and opportunities
36. Charitable contributions

4. STAKEHOLDER RELATIONS
37. Employees
38. Legislators and regulators
39. Local communities
40. Investors
41. Suppliers
42. Consumers
43. Industry Associations
44. Environment groups
45. Science and education
46. Media

5. SUSTAINABLE DEVELOPMENT
47. Global environment
48. Global development
49. Technology co-operation
50. Global standards

APPENDIX XIV
Major environmental problems in selected countries, 1994[*]

Region/ Country	Main environmental problems	Notes
EUROPE		
Austria	Forest degradation	Estimated 25% have suffered some damage.
	New protected areas	Former 'no-man's lands' along Austria's borders with its former Cold War enemies (Hungary, Czech and Slovak republics) may be made into national parks.
Belgium	Water pollution	Highly polluted Meuse River is main source of drinking water. High nitrate concentration, due to agriculture, in some rivers.
	Air pollution	Contributor to Europe's acid rain problem.
Bulgaria	Land contamination	Heavy metal pollution due to metallurgic industry, mining, dumping of waste.
	Water pollution	Raw sewage, heavy metals, nitrates, oil derivatives and detergents pollute most reaches of large rivers.
	Air pollution	Industrial emissions are primary source of the pollutants.
	Threatened forests	Approximately 25% of forests damaged by air pollution.
Denmark	North Sea pollution	Pollution increasing leading to severe algal blooms over past few decades.
	Hazardous waste sites	More than 3,100 old sites thought to contain chemical wastes.
	Pollution from animal manures	Nitrogen in these manures is primary cause of nitrate pollution in waters.
Finland	Air pollution and acid rain	Over 50% of the acidic emission comes from other countries.
	Water pollution	Largely due to pulp and paper mills.
	Endangered species	Since 1950s, 22% of wetlands destroyed, major cause of problem.
France	Water pollution	Industrial pollution, nitrates from agriculture and urban wastes are the main reasons for poor quality of many rivers.
	Air pollution	Vehicle emissions major source in many cities.
	Forest damage	Moderate damage. 20% of forests have suffered some damage.

Germany	Air pollution	SE damaged by pollution from coal-burning utilities and industries. Contributor to acid rain problems. Most cars use leaded gasoline.
	Water pollution	Raw sewage and industrial effluents with heavy metals and toxic chemicals mean poor river quality in eastern areas.
	Forest damage	Acid rain and other pollutants have damaged 50% of trees in eastern and western areas.
Greece	Air pollution	Largely due to vehicle emissions, therefore have established strict laws. Athens is still very polluted, however.
	Water pollution	Severe problems in some gulfs due to industrial effluents, largely untreated, and oil spills and emptying of bilges from tanks and ships in water. Agricultural runoff also a problem.
Italy	Air pollution	Industrial and domestic emissions of sulphur dioxide damage stone monuments and human health. Nitrogen oxide emissions also high.
	Water pollution	Coastal waters and inland rivers polluted by industry, sewage and agriculture.
The Netherlands	Water pollution	Three of Europe's industry-lined rivers (the Rhine, Meuse and Schelde) converge here, carrying enormous quantities of heavy metals, organic compounds and nutrients.
	Air pollution	The Dutch drive the most cars per sq. mile and burn the most fossil fuel per person in Europe. Industrial emissions also a problem.
	Contaminated drinking water	Chemical fertilisers and animal manure have contaminated groundwaters.
Poland	Air pollution	Severe due to coal-fired power plants.
	Water pollution	Industrial and municipal sources of pollutants have increased dramatically. Only 6% of water is considered clean enough for municipal use.
	Forest damage	Severely damaged, 75% show some damage from air pollution.
	Hazardous waste	Most disposed of improperly.
Portugal	Erosion	Poor soil overworked by agriculture.
	Water pollution	Mostly coastal pollution.
	Air pollution	Heavy concentrations of traffic and industry in some areas cause regional problems
	Toxic waste	Only one controlled landfill exists, much of waste improperly disposed of.
Romania	Industrial pollution	Town of Copsa Mica is considered one of the most polluted places in Europe due to only 2 factories.
	Water pollution	85% of main rivers non-potable.
	Soil erosion and degradation	Domestic and industrial waste disposed in uncontrolled manner. Emissions from factories and overuse of chemical fertilisers degrade soils.
	Disaster damage	Since 1970, has suffered 2 floods, 2 large earthquakes and fallout of Chernobyl nuclear accident.

Spain	Air pollution	Major cities have high level of pollution.
	Water pollution	Poor sewage and water treatment facilities, plus agriculture and off-shore oil and gas production.
	Land degradation	Poor soils, irregular rainfall and inefficient farming practices has degraded soils.
	Forest damage	Light damage compared to most European countries.
Sweden	Soil and water acidification	Seriously affected 16,000 lakes. Only 12 percent of all sulphur emission from Swedish sources, most from Germany, Poland.
	Pollution in the North and Baltic seas	Alarming signs of environmental stress seen. In 1988, massive algal bloom caused major fish kill.
Switzerland	Air pollution	Vehicles are prime source of emissions.
	Solid waste	Use mostly incinerators for disposal. Contribute to acid rain also emissions of heavy metals.
	Water pollution	Pollution from agricultural sources increasing.
	Biodiversity	High proportion of plant and animal life vulnerable to habitat destruction and pollution.
United Kingdom	Air pollution	Responsible for 9-12% of sulphur (acid rain ingredient) in Norway. Emissions from large combustion plants a problem as are vehicles.
	Water pollution	Half of serious water pollution from farms. Many of country's beaches contaminated and is one of most significant polluters of North Sea.
	Presence of radon (radiation) in homes	Half total radiation received by humans in UK. About 75,000 houses may require treatment.

NORTH AMERICA

Barbados	Soil erosion	Has shallow soils and lack of vegetative cover, NE region suffers periodic landslides and rock falls, mechanisation of sugar can industry increases problem.
	Coastal pollution	Oil slicks from passing ships a problem.
	Solid waste disposal	Accepts, then incinerates waste from ships calling in at port. Open air burning a problem as are illegal dumping in gullies and old quarries.
Canada	Acid rain	Much of US. origin, has affected 150,000 lakes, productivity of forests reduced.
	Marine habitat destruction	Damaged by agriculture, mining, forestry, urban development, industry and overfishing. Fishing is banned off coast of Newfoundland and restricted around Nova Scotia and British Columbia.
	Forest issues	Clear-cutting, planting stands with single species, and heavy use of pesticides are damaging the resource.
Costa Rica	Deforestation	Forests have been cleared for agriculture and reforestation efforts have been limited.
	Soil erosions	Deforestation has led to land degradation. Forestland converted to pasture in areas with low-fertility on hilly areas where rainfall is heavy increases problem.
Guatemala	Deforestation	Increasing as land is cleared for agriculture, ranching and for domestic fuel. 75% of households use wood for domestic energy needs.
	Biodiversity	Deforestation is reducing habitats and thereby affecting the country's biodiversity

Jamaica	Land degradation	Livestock grazing and subsistence farming reducing productivity of soils.
	Water pollution	Rapid growth of urban area around Kingston has increased problems related to discharge of sewage and industrial effluent.
	Mining pollution	Bauxite mining disturbs large tracts of land. Waste from processing causes air pollution and has contaminated groundwater.
Mexico	Pollution	Air, water and land pollution is severe around industrial areas.
	Deforestation	Forests are being cleared at a substantial rate for agriculture and the growing industrial sector.
	Water scarcity	There is a crucial need for water in much of the country.
United States	Air pollution	Quality is improving but still falls below national standards in many cities.
	Water pollution	Runoff of excess pesticides and fertilisers from farms a threat to rivers, lakes and estuaries.
	Habitat degradation	Continuous loss of old growth forests and wetlands and degradation of other habitats have led to declining waterfowl population and reduced fish populations and overall biodiversity.
	Global warming contribution	The largest single emitter of greenhouse gases. Releases more than 20% of global carbon dioxide emissions from fossil fuel burning.

AFRICA

Algeria	Land degradation	Extensive erosion from farming in marginal areas, overgrazing and destruction of vegetation from gathering of firewood or use as animal fodder.
	Water scarcity	Scarce and drought is common. Poorly maintained water supply systems lead to wasting of this resource and create an urgent need for water conservation efforts. Waterborne diseases a frequent problem.
	Pollution	Untreated urban sewage is a major cause of water pollution and industrial and petroleum refining wastes are often dumped untreated into sewage systems or rivers. In addition, silt from land erosion and oil pollution in coastal water contribute to increasing pollution and overfertilisation of the Mediterranean Sea.
Egypt	Loss of agricultural land	Urban growth encroaching on agricultural land.
	Soil damage and loss	Salinization caused by irrigation has damaged soil. Plus windblown sands and urban sprawl remove arable soils from use.
	Oil pollution	Threatening coral reefs, commercial fisheries, birds, mangroves and coastal and marine resources. Much of coast is coated with tar and petroleum residues.
	Water pollution	Many causes, including runoff of salinized drainage water from irrigated areas, use of pesticides, lack of adequate sewage disposal and industrial effluents.

Ghana	Desertification	NW third of the country faces moderate to serious threat because increased population pressure has led to overgrazing, overcultivation and reduced fallow periods.
	Deforestation	Forest loss is estimated at 278 square miles a year. Inadequate and hazardous supplies of drinking water.
	Water pollution	Pollution by industrial, commercial, domestic and community wastes is common. Existing dams and water conservation practices spread waterborne diseases.
	Wildlife depletion	Enforcement of laws to protect native wild species is poor.
Iran	Deforestation	Only 7,000 square miles of forests remain in the Caspian region and other forests reduced to scattered woods.
	Water pollution	Strait of Hormuz polluted by heavy oil tanker traffic and massive spill during the 1991 Iran/Iraq Gulf War. One of most polluted bodies of water in the world, endangering wildlife including whales, dolphin and bird population.
	Water shortages	Drought – rainfall well below average in recent years. Shortages of drinking water.
	Air pollution	Polluted especially in urban areas by emission from cars, refinery operations and industry.
Iraq	War devastation	Extensive bombardment of Iraq during the Gulf War and movements of tanks and troops have caused extensive damage, particularly to fragile desert soils near Saudi Arabian border.
	Water contamination	Sewage and water treatment facilities also damaged during Gulf War resulting in contamination, especially in Baghdad. Outbreaks of waterborne disease increasing.
Israel	Water scarcity and pollution	Supply is severely limited. Groundwater and surface waters polluted by industrial, domestic and agricultural wastes.
	Coastal resources	Increased by intensive recreational use of areas.
	Air pollution	Power plants, quarries, cement factories and oil refineries are major contributors. Vehicle emissions also a factor.
Kenya	Land degradation	Soil erosion is serious in both fertile and semiarid areas. Up to two million people may be threatened by desertification. High rate of tourism and grazing by wild herbivores causing problems in parks.
	Deforestation	Forests being rapidly lost due to clearance for new agricultural lands or for fuelwood.
	Pollution	Due to urban and industrial waste, some untreated, an increasing problem around Nairobi and Mombasa. Increased use of pesticides and fertilisers also affecting water quality.
Nigeria	Soil degradation	Expanding population creates pressures for land, reducing fallow periods and resulting in erosion. Poor farming techniques and lack of watershed protection contribute to problem.
	Water contamination	Due to poor sanitation and inadequate treatment of sewage coupled with weak regulatory institutions.

	Deforestation	Has lost almost 80% of forest, savannah and wetland areas. Protected areas vulnerable to poaching, illegal logging, farming and grazing due to poor enforcement.
Senegal	Land degradation	Problems with both desertification and deforestation. Fuelwood harvesting, charcoal production and overgrazing by livestock have denuded much of the landscape.
	Wildlife poaching	World's largest exporter of exotic birds. Poaching and overharvesting a problem. Elephant, crocodile and sea turtle populations also suffer from poaching.
	Water development	Project to dam and develop the Senegal River basin threatens to disrupt the ecology of the area.
South Africa	Water quality and supply	Demand likely to outstrip supply by end of decade. Salinization a threat and urban discharge and agricultural runoff have led to eutrophication of most major rivers.
	Soil erosion	Apartheid forced much of population to farm marginal lands. Annual soil losses nationally amount to an estimated 300-400 million tons.
	Air pollution	Severe in Eastern Transvaal Highveld region. Acid precipitation and sulphur oxide emissions are 3-4 times greater than in Germany and UK.
Zimbabwe	Land degradation	Soil erosion is country's most critical problem, especially where marginal land has been forced into overuse.
	Deforestation	Extensive forests are being depleted for firewood and through slash-and-burn agriculture.
	Pollution	Industrialisation has created problems in both urban and rural areas. Several lakes have experienced eutrophication due to discharges of untreated sewage and industrial wastes.

ASIA

Bangladesh	Water regulation	Deforestation of the Himalayas has reduced capacity of the slopes to retain monsoon rains, causing increasingly savage floods in the wet season and inadequate flow in the dry season. Also water table dropping causing water shortages and intrusion of saltwater into cultivated areas.
	Pollution and contamination	Industrial degradation of water and soil plus flood conditions result in the spread of polluted water across areas used for fishing and rice cultivation. Heavy use of pesticides contributes.
	Access to clean water	Many have no access to potable water, therefore waterborne diseases a problem. 17% of children die before age 5 years.
China	Air pollution	In cities is severe enough to threaten health. More cities exceed WHO guidelines for air pollution than in any other country. Coal burning main cause. Acid rain has damaged soils and trees over large parts of the country.
	Water supply and pollution	Severe water shortage in north, which has 64% of cultivated land and only 19% of water. More than one-third lack access to clean water. Industry dumps most of its wastewater without treatment.

	Deforestation	Threatens habitats of natural species, soil erosion and frequent flooding.
	Destruction of grasslands	At least 330,000 square miles show evidence of degradation.
India	Land degradation	Two-thirds of arable land degraded due to overgrazing, deforestation and improper agricultural practices. Also much pressure for fuelwood and livestock fodder. Intensive agriculture and high chemical inputs have depleted nutrients in soils; irrigation causing water-logging and salinization in others.
	Water shortages and pollution	Rainfall is highly seasonal. Large dams are controversial. Over-exploitation of groundwater has caused alarming drop in water tables. Untreated sewage, industrial effluents and excessive use of pesticides and fertilisers pollute most surface waters and some groundwaters.
	Urban pollution	Air pollution levels high in the cities. Not many have access to sewage treatment facilities. Over 30% of urban dwellers live in slums.
	Conserving biodiversity	Pressure on ecosystems due to expanding agriculture, tree plantations and hydrological and mining projects.
Japan	Air and water pollution	Acid rain is a serious problem in many parts of the country and has led to degradation of water quality in many lakes and reservoirs, threatening aquatic life.
	Marine degradation	Overfishing and increasing levels of pollution have begun to reduce the catch. Drift net fishing indiscriminately kills a large number of fish and sea mammals other than those sought by the fishing fleet.
Malaysia	Coastal degradation	Most estuaries are heavily silted and many are no longer productive. Coral reefs are largely absent and mangroves are under threat in all parts of the country. Fish catches have declined due to overfishing.
	Water pollution	Discharges and runoffs from tin mines have polluted 40% of peninsular rivers. Contamination by untreated sewage prevalent along coasts.
	Deforestation	More than half of river basins have been seriously denuded. Logging continues and has sparked a growing number of protests by citizens in forest-dependent communities, particular in Sabah and Sarawak.
Pakistan	Water scarcity and pollution	Almost no excess capacity to meet growing demand for water for irrigation, drinking or for recharging groundwater supplies. Less than 50% have access to safe drinking water; waterborne diseases cause approximately 80% of disease. Untreated industrial effluents and agricultural runoff contribute to pollution.
	Land degradation and deforestation	Population pressure and poor management have caused significant land degradation. Forests shrinking by 1% per year due to cutting for household fuelwood and for agriculture.

	Urban environmental problems	Rapid urbanisation has increased air pollution, congestion, shortages of safe drinking water and housing, and proliferation of squatter settlements. Solid waste is disposed of in open pits or in water.
Philippines	Deforestation and land degradation	Deforestation caused by indiscriminate and often illegal logging, as well as increasing population and agricultural pressures. Deforestation contributes to soil erosion, siltation, flooding, and drought; also degrades habitats rich in biodiversity.
	Coastal degradation	Much of pollution due to natural causes such as excessive rainfall and tropical storms.
	Pollution	Air and soil pollution due to industrial and other toxic wastes. 38 river systems severely polluted.
Thailand	Deforestation	Country is rapidly being denuded due to logging and encroachment by farmers. Natural habitats shrinking due to loss of forests. Wildlife threatened by hunters. Primary causes are the destruction of forested watersheds, poor management of irrigation systems, and inefficient water use.
	Industrial pollution	Industrial pollution, air pollution, an inadequate sewage system and traffic congestion are serious problems.

OCEANIA

Australia	Land degradation	Inappropriate use of land is wide-spread and has resulted in soil salinity and loss of native vegetation.
	Endangered species	Many species at risk due to loss of habitat and competition or predation from introduced species.
New Zealand	Impacts of introduced species	Settlers brought with them plants, animal and insects which are having a serious impact on native species, particularly birds.
	Ownership of natural resources	A treaty gave Maori chiefs rights to vast tracts of land. There are major uncertainties about property rights and natural resource and environmental management authority.
	Deforestation	Only one third of original forest remains, although commercial stocks are growing.
Solomon Islands	Deforestation	Careless logging operations are damaging large areas of forests and policing is inefficient. Heavy rains make exposed soils vulnerable to erosion. Farming on steep slopes and deforestation are major causes of erosion.

SOUTH AMERICA

Argentina	Air and water pollution	Has a heavily concentrated population in major cities leading to air and water pollution. Increased use of pesticides and fertilisers damaging water quality.
	Waste disposal	Few laws on the disposal of hazardous and nuclear wastes. Need clear and proper management over environmental threats to public health.
	Soil erosion	Heavy flooding is a problem near rivers. Adequate flood control is needed, damage exacerbated by improper land use practices.

Brazil	Deforestation	The major cutting and burning campaigns of the 1980s are now under better control, but still lose millions of acres of tropical forest each year.
	Water pollution	Serious river pollution near cities is common due to dumping of untreated sewage and industrial wastes. Also mercury wastes in gold-mining areas.
	Land degradation	Very poor soils in Amazon region are washed away when trees are cut. Shortages of land push farmers onto marginal or steeply sloping lands which erode easily.
Chile	Deforestation and soil erosion	Strong and expanding forestry industry. Misuse of forests leading to soil erosion, biodiversity loss and water pollution.
	Water pollution	Competition for water amongst agricultural, mining and urban using is increasing and beginning to pose serious environmental threats. Watershed damage exacerbates problem.
	Overfishing	Without controls, fish catches are likely to decline precipitously.
Colombia	Land degradation	Large areas have been cleared for cattle raising, coffee production and mining, resulting in soil erosion. Heavy rains and poor land use practice cause soil to be washed away.
	Deforestation	Over-exploitation of tropical hardwoods, pines and eucalyptus trees.
	Endangered species.	As a result of deforestation, some 1,000 species of plants and 24 animals species are threatened with extinction. Two-thirds of native bird species also endangered.
Peru	Soil degradation	Most of Peru's land contains poor-quality soil that is easily degraded. Centuries of grazing plus recent logging in forests threaten soil productivity and increase erosion.
	Overfishing and marine pollution	Overfishing by native and foreign fleets has slowed the recovery of the anchovy fishery. Pollution of coastal waters by industrial and municipal wastes and poisonous mine tailings are increasing the problem.
Venezuela	Deforestation and soil degradation	Lost an average of 1,000 square miles of forest per year in the 1980s. Land is overgrazed and degraded, leading to erosion and compaction.
	Urban and industrial pollution	Sewage treatment is scarce and industrial pollution controls are few and poorly enforced. Problem most severe along Caribbean coast.
	Freshwater pollution	Both major lakes are significantly polluted due to urban sewage, oil and mining wastes.

* Adapted from World Resources Institute (compilers), *The 1994 Information Please Environmental Almanac,* Houghton Mifflin Company, 222 Berkeley Street, Boston, Massachussets, USA 012116-3764, 1994, pp. 374-681.

APPENDIX XV
Contact organisations and addresses

Regulatory bodies

AEA Technology
National Environmental Technology Centre
Culham
Abingdon
Oxfordshire
OX14 3DB
Tel: 01235 463072   Fax: 01235 463011

Department of the Environment
South East
2 Marsham Street
London
SW1P 3EB
Tel: 0171 276 3000   Fax: 0171 276 0818

Department of Trade and Industry
South East Division
Ashdown House
123 Victoria Street
London
SW1E 6RB
Tel: 0171 215 5000   Fax: 0171 222 2629

Department of Transport
2 Marsham Street
London
SW1P 3EB
Tel: 0171 271 5000   Fax: 0171 271 4377

Energy Efficiency Office
South East
2 Marsham Street
London
SW1P 3EB
Tel: 0171 276 6200   Fax: 0171 276 3706

Energy Technology Support Unit (ETSU)
Energy Efficiency Enquiries Bureau
Harwell
Oxfordshire
OX11 0RA
Tel: 01235 436747   Fax: 01235 433066

Environment Agency
Head Office
Rivers House
Waterside Drive
Aztec West
Almondsbury
Bristol
BS12 4UD
Tel: 01454 624400   Fax: 01454 624409

Environment Agency
Anglian Regional Office
Kingfisher House
Goldhay Way
Orton Goldhay
Peterborough
PE2 5ZR
Tel: 01733 371811   Fax: 01733 231840

Environment Agency
Northeastern Regional Office
Rivers House
21 Park Square South
Leeds
LS1 2QG
Tel: 01132 440191   Fax: 01132 461889

Environment Agency
Northwestern Regional Office
Richard Fairclough House
Knutsford Road
Warrington
WA4 1HG
Tel: 01925 653999   Fax: 01925 415961

Environment Agency
Midlands Regional Office
Sapphire East
550 Streetsbrook Road
Solihull
B91 1QT
Tel: 0121 7112324   Fax: 0121 7115824

Environment Agency
Southern Regional Office
Guildbourne house
Chatsworth Road
Worthing
West Sussex
Tel: 01903 820692   Fax: 01903 821832

Environment Agency
Southwestern Regional Office
Manley House
Kestrel Way
Exeter
EX2 7LQ
Tel: 01392 444000   Fax: 01392 444238

Environment Agency
Thames Regional Office
Kings Meadow House
Kings Meadow Road
Reading
RG1 8DQ
Tel: 01734 535000   Fax: 01734 500388

Environment Agency
Welsh Regional Office
Rivers House/Plas-yr-Afon
St Mellons Business Park
St Mellons
Cardiff
CF3 0LT
Tel: 01222 770088   Fax: 01222 798555

European Environment Agency (EEA)
Kongens Nytorv 6
DK-1050 Copenhagen K
Denmark
Tel: +45 33 36 71 00

Heath and Safety Executive
Broad Lane
Sheffield
S3 7H1
Tel: 01742 872000   Fax: 01742 892000

International Martime Organization (IMO)
Marine Environment Division
4 Albert Embankment
London
SE1 7SR
Tel: 0171 735 7611   Fax: 0171 537 3210

Ministry of Agriculture, Fisheries and Food
Whitehall Place
London
SW1A 2HH
Tel: 0171 270 8080

National Radiological Protection Board
Chilton
Didcot
Oxfordshire
OX11 0RQ
Tel: 01235 831600   Fax: 01235 833891

Royal Commission on Environmental Pollution
Church House
Great Smith Street
London
SW1P 3BZ
Tel: 0171 276 2080   Fax: 0171 276 2098

Scottish Environment Protection Agency (SEPA)
Head Office
Erksine Court
The Castle Business Park
Stirling
FK9 4TR
Tel: 01786 457700   Fax: 01786 446885

SEPA
North Region HQ
Graesser House
Fodderty Way
Dingwall
IV15 9XB
Tel: 01349 862021   Fax: 01349 863987

SEPA
West Region HQ
Rivers House
Murray Road
East Kilbride
G75 0LA
Tel: 01355 238181   Fax: 01355 264323

SEPA
East Region HQ
Clearwater House
Heriot-Watt Research Park
Avenue North
Riccarton
Edinburgh
EH14 4AP
Tel: 0131 449 7296   Fax: 0131 449 7277

United Nations Environment Programme (UNEP)
PO Box 30552
Nairobi
Kenya
Tel: +254 233 3930

United Nations Environment Programme Industry and Environment (UNEPIE)
Industry and Environment Office
Tour Mirabeau
39-43, quai Andre Citroen,
F-75739 Paris Cedex 15
France
Tel: +33 1 40 58 88 50   Fax: +33 1 40 58 88 74

United States of America Environmental Protection Agency (USEPA)
401 M Street SW
Washington, D.C.
USA
20460
Tel: +1-202 382 4700

Water Companies

Anglian Water Plc
Anglian House
Ambury Road
Cambridgeshire
PE18 6NZ
Tel: 01480 443000   Fax: 01480 443115

Anglian Water Services Ltd
Compass House
Chivers Way
Histon
Cambridge
CB4 4ZY
Tel: 01223 372000   Fax: 01223 372166

Biwater supply (Holdings) Plc
Biwater House
Station Approach
Dorking
Surrey
RH4 1TZ
Tel: 01306 740740   Fax: 01306 885233

Bournemouth Water Plc
Knapp Mill, Mill Road
Christchurch
Dorset
BH23 2LU
Tel: 01202 499000   Fax: 01202 499100

Bristol Water Plc
P O Box 218
Bridgwater Road
Bristol
BS99 7AU
Tel: 01179 665881   Fax: 01179 634576

Cambridge Water Company
41 Rustat Road
Cambridge
CB1 3QS
Tel: 01223 247351   Fax: 01223 214052

Chester Waterworks Company
Aqua House
45 Boughton
Chester
CH3 5AU
Tel: 01244 320501   Fax: 01244 316192

Cholderton and District Water Co Ltd
Estate Office
Cholderton
Salisbury
Wiltshire
SP4 0DR
Tel: 01980 629203   Fax: 01980 629307

The Colne Valley Water Company Plc
Blackwell House
Aldenham
Watford
Hertfordshire
WD2 2EY
Tel: 01923 223333   Fax: 01923 249395

Dwr Cymru Welsh Water
Plas Y Ffynnon
Cambrian Way
Brecon
Powys
LD3 7HP
Tel: 01874 623181   Fax: 01874 624167

East Surrey Water Plc
London Road
Redhill
Surrey
RH1 1LJ
Tel: 01737 765933   Fax: 01737 766807

Eastbourne Water Company
14 Upperton Road
Eastbourne
Sussex
BN21 1EP
Tel: 01323 411411   Fax: 01323 411412

Essex Water Copmany
Hall Street
Chelmsford
Essex
CM2 0HH
Tel: 01245 212236   Fax: 01245 212345

Folkestone and Dover Services Ltd
The Cherry Garden
Cherry Garden Lane
Folkestone
Kent
CT19 4QB
Tel: 01303 276951   Fax: 01303 276712

G U Projects Ltd
Blackwell House
Aldenham Road
Watford
Hertfordshire
WD2 2LG
Tel: 01923 814291   Fax: 01923 814398

Hamdden Ltd
Plas Y Ffynnon
Cambrian Way
Brecon
Powys
LD3 7HP
Tel: 01874 623181   Fax: 01874 624167

Hartlepool Water Company
3 Lancaster Road
Hartlepool
TS24 8LW
Tel: 01429 274405   Fax: 01429 278961

Lee Valley Water Plc
P O Box 48
Bishops Rise
Hartfield
Hertfordshire
AL10 9HL
Tel: 01707 268111   Fax: 01707 268970

Mid Southern Water Company
22 – 30 Sturt Court
Firmley Green
Camberley
Surrey
GU16 6HZ
Tel: 01252 835031   Fax: 01252 836066

North East Water Plc
P O Box 10
Allendale Road
Newcastle Upon Tyne
NE6 2SW
Tel: 0191 265 4144   Fax: 0191 267 6612

North Surrey Water Ltd
Millis House
The Causeway
Staines
Middlesex
TW18 3BX
Tel: 01784 455464   Fax: 01784 451260

North West Water Group Plc (Part of United Utilities)
Dawson House
Liverpool Road,
Great Sankey
Warrington
Cheshire
WA5 3LW
Tel: 01925 234000   Fax: 01925 233360

North West Water Ltd
Dawson House
Liverpool Road,
Great Sankey
Warrington
Cheshire
WA5 3LW
Tel: 01925 234000   Fax: 01925 233382

Northumbrian Water Group Plc
Regent Centre
Gosforth
Newcastle Upon Tyne
NE3 3PX
Tel: 0191 284 3151   Fax: 0191 284 0378

Northumbrian Water Ltd
Abbey Road
Pity Me
Durham
County Durham
DH1 5FJ
Tel: 0191 383 2222   Fax: 0191 383 1209

Portsmouth Water Plc
P O Box 8
West Street
Havant
Hampshire
PO9 1LG
Tel: 01705 499888   Fax: 01705 453632

Rickmansworth Water Plc
London Road
Rickmansworth
Hertfordshire
WD3 1LB
Tel: 01923 776633   Fax: 01923 896263

Saur UK
22 – 30 Sturt Road
Firmley Green
Camberley
Surrey
GU16 6HZ
Tel: 01252 837639   Fax: 01252 838370

Saur Water Services Plc
22 – 30 Sturt Road
Firmley Green
Camberley
Surrey
GU16 6HZ
Tel: 01252 837639   Fax: 01252 838370

Severn Trent Plc
2308 Coventry Road
Birmingham
B26 3JZ
Tel: 0121 722 6000   Fax: 0121 722 6132

Severn Trent Water Ltd
2297 Coventry Road
Sheldon
Birmingham
B26 3PU
Tel: 0121 722 4000   Fax: 0121 722 4800

South East Water
14 Upperton Road
Eastbourne
Sussex
BN21 1EP
Tel: 01323 649207   Fax: 01323 648237

South Staffordshire Water Plc
Green Lane
Walsall
West Midlands
WS2 7PD
Tel: 01922 38282   Fax: 01922 725542

South West Water Plc
Peninsula House
Rydon Lane
Exeter
Devon
EX2 7HR
Tel: 01392 446688   Fax: 01392 443912

Southern Water Plc
Southern House
Yeoman Road
Worthing
Sussex
BN13 3NX
Tel: 01903 264444   Fax: 01903 262147

Suffolk Water Company Plc
P O Box 1
Lowestoft
Suffolk
NR32 5JT
Tel: 01502 572406   Fax: 01502 572406

Sutton District Water Co
59 Gander Green Lane
Cheam
Sutton
Surrey
SM1 2EW
Tel: 0181 643 8050   Fax: 0181 643 4461

Tendring Hundred Services Ltd
Mill Hill
Manningtree
Essex
CO11 2AZ
Tel: 01206 392155   Fax: 01206 395541

Thames Water Plc
14 Cavendish Place
London
W1M 9DJ
Tel: 0171 636 8686   Fax: 0171 436 6752

Three Valleys Water Services Plc
P O Box 48
Bishops Rise
Hatfield
Hertfordshire
AL10 9HL
Tel: 01707 268111   Fax: 01707 268970

Welsh Water Plc
Plas Y Ffynnon
Cambrian Way
Breacon
Powys
LD3 7HP
Tel: 01874 623181   Fax: 01874 624167

Wessex Water Plc
Wessex House
Passage Street
Bristol
BS2 0JQ
Tel: 01179 290611   Fax: 01179 293137

West Hampshire Water Plc
Knapp Mill
Water Mill Road
Christchurch
Dorset
BH23 2LU
Tel: 01202 499000   Fax: 01202 499100

Wrexham and East Denbighshire Water Co
Packsaddle Depot
Wrexham Road, Rhostyllen
Wrexham
Clwyd
LL14 4DS
Tel: 01978 846946   Fax: 01978 846888

The York Waterworks Plc
Lendal Tower
York
North Yorkshire
YO1 2DL
Tel: 01904 622171   Fax: 01904 611667

Yorkshire Water Services Ltd
West Riding House
67 Albion Street
Leeds
LS1 5AA
Tel: 01132 448201   Fax: 01132 443071

Yorkshire Waterlink
114 Harrogate Road
Leeds
LS7 4NY
Tel: 01132 682818   Fax: 01132 663131

Trade Associations

Association for Consumer Research
2 Marylebone Road
London
NW1 4DF
Tel: 0171 830 6000   Fax: 0171 935 1606

Association of British Certification Bodies
10th Floor Norfolk House
Wellesley Road
Croydon
Surrey
CR9 2DT
Tel: 0181 680 1822   Fax: 0181 681 8146

Association of Consulting Engineers
Alliance House
12 Caxton Street
London
SW1H 0QL
Tel: 0171 222 6557   Fax: 0171 222 0750

Association of Environmental Consultancies
P O Box 472
St Albans
Hertfordshire
AL1 1AD
Tel: 01727 853498   Fax: 01727 850553

British Effluent and Water Association
5 Castle Street
High Wycombe
Buckinghamshire
HP13 6RZ
Tel: 01494 444544   Fax: 01494 446185

British Print Industries Federation
11 Bedford Row
London
WC1R 4DX
Tel: 0171 242 6904   Fax: 0171 405 7784

British Recovered Paper Association
Papermakers House
Rivenhall Road
Westlea
Swindon
SN5 7BD
Tel: 01793 886086   Fax: 01793 886182

Chemical Industries Association
Kings Building
Smith Square
London
SW1P 3JJ
Tel: 0171 834 3399   Fax: 0171 834 4469

Combined Heat and Power Association
Grovesnor Gardens House
35 – 37 Grovesnor Gardens
London
SW1W 0BS
Tel: 0171 828 4077   Fax: 0171 828 0310

Confederation of British Industry
Centre Point
103 New Oxford Street
London
WC1A 1DU
Tel: 0171 379 7400   Fax: 0171 836 1114

Institute of Energy
18 Devonshire Street
London
W1N 2AU
Tel: 0171 580 7124   Fax: 0171 580 4420

Institute of Environmental Assessment
Fen Road
East Kirkby
Lincolnshire
PE23 4DB
Tel: 01790 763613   Fax: 01790 763630

Institute of Environmental Management
58-59 Timber Bursh
Edinburgh
EH6 6QH
Tel: 0131 555 5334   Fax: 0131 555 5217

Institute of Environmental Sciences
14 Princes Gate
London
SW7 1PU
Tel: 0181 766 6755

Institute of Water and Environmental Management
16 John Street
London
WC1N 2EB
Tel: 0171 831 3110   Fax: 0171 405 4967

Non-Governmental Organisations (NGOs)

British Trust for Conservation Volunteers
36 St Mary's Street
Wallingford
Oxfordshire
OX10 0EU
Tel: 01491 39766   Fax: 01491 39646

British Trust for Ornithology (BTO)
The National Centre for Ornithology
The Nunnery
Thetford
Norfolk
IP24 2PU
Tel: 01842 750050   Fax: 01842 750030

Business in the Environment
8/9 Stratton Street
London
W1X 5FD
Tel: 0171 629 1600   Fax: 0171 629 1834

Centre of Exploitation of Science and Technology
5 Berners Road
London
N1 0PW
Tel: 0171 354 9942   Fax: 0171 354 4301

The Conservation Foundation
1 Kensington Gore
London
SW7 2AR
Tel: 0171 823 8842   Fax: 0171 823 8791

Council for the Protection of Rural England
Warwick House
25 Buckingham Palace Road
London
SW1W 0PP
Tel: 0171 976 6433   Fax: 0171 976 6373

Earthwatch Europe
Belsyre Court
57 Woodstock Road
Oxford
OX2 6HU
Tel: 01865 311600   Fax: 01865 311383

The Environmental Council
21 Elizabeth Street
London
SW1W 9RP
Tel: 0171 824 8411   Fax: 0171 730 9941

Friends of the Earth
26 – 28 Underwood Street
London
N1 7JQ
Tel: 0171 490 1555   Fax: 0171 490 0881

Green Alliance
2nd Floor
49 Wellington Street
London
WC2E 7BN
Tel: 0171 836 0341   Fax: 0171 240 9205

Greenpeace
Canonbury Villas
London
N1 2PN
Tel: 0171 354 5100   Fax: 0171 696 0014

Joint Nature Conservation Committee (JNCC)
Monkstone House
City Road
Peterborough
PE1 1JY
Tel: 01733 562626   Fax: 01733 555948

Royal Society for the Protection of Birds (RSPB)
The Lodge
Sandy
Bedfordshire
SG19 2DL
Tel: 01767 680551   Fax: 01767 692365

UK Centre For Economic and Environmental Development
3E Kings Parade
Cambridge
Cambridgeshire
CB2 1SJ
Tel: 01223 67799   Fax: 01223 67794

Women's Environmental Network (WEN)
Aberdeen Studios
22 Highbury Grove
London
N5 2EA
Tel: 0171 354 8823   Fax: 0171 354 0464

World Conservation Monitoring Centre (WCMC)
219c Hutingdon Road
Cambridge
CB3 0DL
Tel: 01223 277314   Fax: 01223 277136

World Wide Fund For Nature
Weyside Park, Panda House
Catteshall Lane
Godalming
Surrey
GU7 1XR
Tel: 01483 426444   Fax: 01483 426409

INDEX

Maastricht Treaty 36
Madagascar 16
MAFF *see* Ministry of Agriculture, Fisheries and Food
Magistrates 39
Magistrates' Courts 2 43
MFN *see* Most Favoured Nation
Ministry of Agriculture, Fisheries and Food (MAFF) 32
Monitoring 49
Most Favoured Nation (MFN) 57

Nagasaki 26
National Power 19
National Rivers Authority (NRA) (*see also* Environment Agency) 12 17 31 33 41 42 44
Natural History Museum (NHM) 66 68
Negligence 35 38
Netherlands 9 18
New Mexico 29
NFFO *see* Non-Fossil Fuel Obligation
NGOs *see* non-governmental agencies
NHM *see* Natural History Museum
NIMBY 29
Noise 24
Non-Fossil Fuel Obligation (NFFO) 20
Non-governmental agencies (NGOs) 5 6
North Sea 15 24
Norway 27
NRA *see* National Rivers Authority
Nuclear energy 21
Nuisance 35

OECD *see* Organization for Economic Cooperation and Development
Organization for Economic Cooperation and Development (OECD) 5 17 18 19
Orimulsion 19 20

PCBs *see* Polychlorinated biphenyls
Penalties 1 2 8 38 39 40 43
PER *see* Polluting Emissions Register
Permits 3 18
Petrol 8 22 86
Piper Alpha 1 15
Polluter Pays Principle 3
Polluting Emissions Register (PER) 50
Polychlorinated biphenyls (PCBs) 29 86
PowerGen 19
Process-related guidance notes 34
Prosecutions 2 40 43
Public health 1 7 12

Radiation 25 26 31 73
Rail transport 22
Recycling 30

The Environmental Information Service

The environment is frequently in the news with Government, business and the general public seriously concerned about many issues. From global issues, such as greenhouse warming and ozone depletion, to local concerns about litter and recycling of waste, the environment is something that concerns everyone.

Whatever the issue, the British Library's Environmental Information Service (EIS) can help researchers to find the information they need - providing hard data, news and contacts.

Environmental Information Service

Enquiries: 0171-412 7955

Fax: 0171-412 7954

Email: eis@bl.uk

Service available: Monday to Friday 09.30-17.00

The Environmental Information Service homepage can be found at **http://portico.bl.uk/sris/eis/**

The Collections

The British Library offers a unique collection of environmental information in its London and Boston Spa reading rooms. The most extensive range of printed and electronic sources is available at the Holborn and Aldwych reading rooms of the Science Reference and Information Service (SRIS).

Holborn Reading Room

25 Southampton Buildings
London WC2A 1AW
Tel: 0171-412 7494/96
Fax: 0171-412 7495
Email: sris-centre-desk@bl.uk

The collections cover the physical and technical sciences and offer material on such topics as:

- Radioactive hazards
- Noise measurement and control
- Pollution of land, water and atmosphere
- Waste management and recycling
- Clean technologies
- Transport and energy
- Science and technology policy
- Contacts within companies, consultancies and organisations

Business and patent information is also available.

Reading Room opening hours: Monday to Friday 09.30-21.00, Saturday 10.00-13.00

Aldwych Reading Room

9 Kean Street
London WC2B 4AT
Tel: 0171-412 7288
Fax: 0171-412 7217
Email: sris-aldwych-desk@bl.uk

The collections cover the life sciences and technologies, (including medicine and mathematics) and offer material on such topics as:

- Impact of chemicals and pollution on plants, animals and human health
- Agriculture and forestry
- Biodiversity and conservation
- Air and water quality
- Climatic change
- Genetically manipulated organisms

The Aldwych Reading Room also offers a number of environmental CD-ROMs including Environmental Abstracts, CAB and BIOSIS.

Reading Room opening hours: Monday to Friday 09.30-17.30

The world's leading resource for scholarship, research and innovation

The Environmental Information Service

The Services

The British Library provides a range of specialist free and priced information services to answer users' needs.

Quick Environmental Enquiry Line
Tel: 0171-412 7955
Fax: 0171-412 7954
Email: eis@bl.uk

This **free** service provides answers on quick queries such as:

- Names and addresses of environmental organisations, suppliers and specialists
- Lists of books, reports, journals and maps held by the British Library
- How to obtain documents
- What information is available on the Internet

Service available: Monday to Friday 09.30-17.00

STMsearch Research Service
Tel: 0171-412 7477
Fax: 0171-412 7954
Email: stm-search@bl.uk

STMsearch provides an in-depth, **fee-based** research service using the widest range of online, CD-ROM and printed sources. It covers all environmental subjects and related areas of science, technology and medicine. With skilled searchers and access to over 400 databases the service provides targeted and comprehensive access to information and a cost-effective solution to research problems.

STMsearch has access to all major environmental databases. Popular databases include Enviroline, Environmental Bibliography, Aqualine, Pollution Abstracts, ECDIN, Oceanic Abstracts, Toxline and CAB Abstracts. Examples of typical searches include:

- Environmental baseline data for Azerbaijan
- Photodegradation of pesticides in soil
- Treatments for sewage sludge

Initial consultations are free and customers are given a quotation before STMsearch undertakes the work. The service aims to deliver the results of a search within five working days of a confirmed request, but faster turn-round times can be negotiated.

Service available: Monday to Friday 09.30-17.00

Training Courses

EIS offers training courses on finding and using environmental information:

Sources of Environmental Information is a day-long course of talks, demonstrations and practical sessions, introducing participants to essential printed sources and electronic information on commercial hosts, CD-ROMs and the Internet. Invited speakers give overviews of information use in a number of practical applications.

Environmental Information on the Internet is a half-day course with introductory talks followed by an extended practical session in which participants are able to discover the Internet for themselves with guidance from library and IT professionals.

For more information
Tel: 0171-412 7470
Fax: 0171-412 7947
Email: sris-customer-services@bl.uk

Document Supply

The British Library Document Supply Centre (DSC) provides the most comprehensive photocopy/loan service in the world. DSC has unrivalled collections of journals, books, conference proceedings, theses and reports. Customers can order material direct and users of STMsearch can take advantage of special discounts.

For more information
Tel: 01937 546060
Fax: 01937 546333
Email: dsc-customer-services@bl.uk

The world's leading resource for scholarship, research and innovation